The International Student Handbook

A Legal Guide to Studying, Working, and Living in the United States

By
Allan Wernick

American Immigration Law Foundation

American Immigration Law Foundation
1400 Eye Street, NW, Suite 1200, Washington, DC 20005
Attn: Publications Director

Printed in the United States of America

ISBN 1-878677-42-X

ACKNOWLEDGMENTS

Writing a book designed to be simple is not a simple task. It involves research, writing, reviewing, rewriting, marketing, and a host of other important contributing activities. Many of my colleagues and friends are deserving of recognition for their assistance and support.

Lynn Neugebauer assisted with the initial research and writing for much of the first draft; Frances Berger also helped with the writing of portions of the first draft. The support of my other co-workers at Wernick & Berger — Nancy Chen, Winnie Chan, Tracey Dean, Arita Winter, and Helena Hungria — were invaluable with their support and assistance.

Peter Rubie, an author, journalist and editor, helped make the Handbook understandable. A job which is not easy when the writing of lawyers is involved.

Amy Novick, Nelson Chipman, David Neal, Elke Powell, and Susan Quarles working on behalf of the American Immigration Law Foundation are to be commended for their work in seeing the Handbook through to publication. AILF should be proud to have them on board.

Special thanks goes to Mariam Cheikh-Ali, Assistant Director of International Student Affairs at Pratt Institute, Brooklyn, New York, a remarkable woman with an outstanding grasp of the law, who gave me invaluable assistance by reviewing this Handbook. Almost all of her numerous suggestions and corrections were incorporated into the text.

I would not have been in a position to write this Handbook if not for Judith Bauduy, Director of International Education at Pace University, New York City, who first introduced me to the world of international students, helping me understand their needs and concerns, allowing me into their lives.

I would also like to thank many of the other Foreign Student Advisors and International Student Service providers in the New

York area who have inspired my continued interest in the concerns of international students in the United States. They include: Nydia Edgecombe, Hostos Community College (CUNY), Rick Tudisco, Ellen Cohen, Sally Taylor, and Beth Mugler, Columbia University; Maria Jacobsen and Elizabeth Barnum, CUNY Graduate Center; June Sadowski-Devarez, St. John's University; Elinor Spiegel, International House, Kathy Postma, Lehman College (CUNY); Nadia Merzliakow, Pratt University; Linda Robinson, Queens College, CUNY; Sal Longarino, Lisa Vogel and Nancy Young, New York University; Len Tolchinsky, Office of Admission Services, CUNY; Bill O'Connell, LaGuardia Community College, CUNY; Gaylene Kauffman and Mary Todesca, Fordham University; Helen Leonard, Center of English Studies; and Casmore Slaw, Technical Career Institute.

Thanks to Adam Green, a noted expert on immigration law, particularly as it impacts on foreign students, at the law firm of Sullivan & Worcester in Boston, for encouraging and supporting my involvement with the foreign student advisor community.

I also wish to thank Ed Rubin at the firm of Rubin & Dornbaum, Newark, New Jersey; Alan Musgrave at the firm of Palmer & Dodge, Boston, Massachusetts; and Greg Adams at the firm of Foster & Jacobs, Cincinnati, Ohio, for their comments on a draft of Part One of the Handbook; and to Phyllis Jewell at the firm of Fallon, Bixby & Cheng in San Francisco, California for answering what seemed to be an unending number of questions on immigration law and policy. Their expert assistance added greatly to the quality of this work. Of course, all final decisions regarding content were my own and I alone am responsible.

The Office of International Education and Services at the University of Iowa allowed us to use substantial portions of their *Handbook for Foreign Students and Scholars*. Their text, with some changes and additions by me, makes up much of Part II. Their generosity reflects a spirit of cooperation which others would do well to emulate. The quality of their work reflects their commitment to excellence.

Allan Wernick
December 1992

INTRODUCTION

You want to study in the United States and maybe supplement your expenses by working. You are about to graduate college, the time the U.S. government has allowed you to stay here as a student is about to run out, and you want to get a green card (become a permanent resident of the United States). All these things involve complicated rules and regulations. Even knowing your basic rights and responsibilities as a foreign student and how to cope with day to day living in the United States requires special knowledge of U.S. laws and customs.

With these kinds of questions in mind, this Handbook was written to provide a current or potential international student with a basic understanding of U.S. immigration law, as well as some basic information about surviving in America.

It is divided into two parts. Part I demystifies and provides an overview of U.S. immigration rules and regulations. While it is written to guide the student, others — including foreign student advisors, college administrators, professors, and attorneys — will also find it useful. Part II provides "lifestyle" information beyond the area of immigration law. It includes such things as understanding U.S. civil and criminal court procedures, understanding an apartment lease, and what you need to know about medical insurance, among other things. We have also included a list of common colloquial, academic terms in the appendix.

U.S. immigration law is dynamic. The laws and regulations change frequently, sometimes even day to day. That is why it is important to view this Handbook as an introduction to the law, not the final word. U.S. law is also filled with subtleties and distinctions, so if the Handbook indicates it is likely that something you want to do is difficult or impossible, check with an expert before giving up. Remember that this Handbook is in no way meant to be a comprehensive overview or to replace the advice of an attorney or foreign student advisor. You will hopefully gain a basic understanding of the legal issues involved, and become sufficiently informed to at least head in the right direction and avoid some of the pitfalls involved in this complicated area of law. For those wishing more detailed information on the law, we have provided a bibliography of relevant materials.

In the Handbook, we use the term international or foreign student to refer to people who are or wish to have lawful status in the United States for the purpose of studying in a college, university, or technical or vocational school. Actually, non-U.S. citizens can study in the United States at every level, including high school. Many foreign students in our U.S. colleges and universities have no lawful status at all, having entered or remained in the United States in violation of our immigration laws.

We address the concerns of people who may be in the United States for the primary purpose of studying in three categories: F-1 student; M-1, student; and J-1 exchange visitor. F-1 status is for pre-college, and most college and university students, M-1 is for technical or vocational school students, and J-1 is for individuals coming to study or work in a special exchange visitor program. The Handbook discusses how a person becomes a foreign student in each of these categories including how best to apply for a visa or change of status, how a person can work while a foreign student, post-graduate employment opportunities, temporary and permanent, and the special problem of J-1 exchange visitors. It also briefly reviews other nonimmigrant visas for investors, intracompany transferees, and visitors.

Understanding U.S. immigration law will help you get into the United States and stay here legally, but there are other things besides your visa and your education to deal with, including finding affordable housing, managing your money, and understanding other legal matters such taxes which preoccupy international students. This Handbook provides a wealth of valuable information designed to ease your mind about living in the U.S.A.

We hope that you find this Handbook both informative and useful.

TABLE OF CONTENTS

PART II

PART
I

PART

I

CHAPTER ONE

The F-1 College and University Student

In order to qualify as an F-1 college or university student, you must be accepted by an accredited institution and establish that you have enough money to study in the United States without working. You must also establish that you do not intend to immigrate to the United States (see more on this in Chapter Two), that you haven't abandoned and do not intend to abandon your residence abroad and, with some exceptions, have a valid passport.

ACCEPTANCE BY A SCHOOL, COLLEGE, OR UNIVERSITY

As a prospective student, you will be required to meet an admissions standard set by the institution for its international students. Nonetheless, some schools are easy to get into, while others — particularly the United States' most prestigious universities — are much harder. You should call or write to any school you are interested in attending, read its catalogue, and follow the application procedures carefully.

Many colleges and universities require a prospective foreign student to take the Test of English as a Foreign Language or "TOEFL" as part of the application process, unless the student is from a country where English is the native language. Thus, Australian and British students will not be asked to take the TOEFL, but students from India or Kenya may be required to take the test. Schools that offer classes in the student's own language, or offer classes in the English language, do not usually require the TOEFL.

FORM I-20

Once you are accepted for admission, you are issued a Form I-20 by the college or university, and this form serves as evidence that the school has admitted you. (A copy of the form appears in the appendix.) Before issuing Form I-20, the school must make sure that you have sufficient financial resources to study full-time without working illegally.

EVIDENCE OF FINANCIAL SUPPORT

While an F-1 student may work in the United States under certain circumstances (see Chapter Five), you must first establish that you can support yourself and pay for both your tuition and living expenses without working illegally. The money can be from your own funds or those of close family members. Since living and studying in the United States can be expensive, a very important part of applying for F-1 status is providing evidence of financial support.

Form I-20 indicates the estimated cost of one year's study at your school. If you apply for F-1 status, you are required to show that you can pay the cost of the first year of study in the United States, and that you have dependable financial resources for the rest of your educational program.

Proof of financial support can be demonstrated in several ways.

Some applicants use what is known as an "Affidavit of Support" or Form I-134. This Affidavit of Support is usually completed by someone in your immediate family such as a parent, brother, or sister, and should be dated less than six months from the date of submission.

In addition to the Affidavit of Support, you need letters from a bank, tax records, or other evidence confirming the financial resources of whomever signs your Affidavit of Support. An Affidavit of Support from someone other than a member of your immediate family may be presented, but it's usually not very helpful.

If you want to prove that you have the personal resources to pay for your own education, you need to show that you can maintain yourself financially throughout the entire period of study. Evidence of bank accounts, a trust, or similar income must be presented.

If a distant relative or friend will support you, it's best for the money to be put directly into your personal bank account rather than rely on an Affidavit of Support. Any factors that can reduce your expenses, such as free room and board, should also be presented to establish your ability to support yourself without working.

The story of Mary:

Mary, from Ireland, wants to study in the United States. She has been admitted to a very prestigious public university in Texas with reasonable tuition fees. Despite the relatively low cost for tuition, however, Mary's family will have great difficulty showing that they can support her without her having to work. The college figures room and board to be $7,000 per student, plus $8,000 tuition for non-residents of the state, for a total of $15,000 a year. Even though Mary's father is an engineer, between Mary and

PURITANO

her two young brothers, $15,000 per year is just a little bit more than the family in Ireland can afford. Mary is fortunate, however. Her older sister lives in the same city where the university is located and has offered to let Mary stay with her throughout her college years. Mary will have her own room and free meals. Mary's sister also will be giving her $50 per week for transportation and entertainment expenses. The only expenses that the father back in Ireland will have to pay will be the tuition fees and Mary's clothing, books, and other miscellaneous expenses. By submitting an affidavit (or sworn statement) from Mary's sister, combined with an affidavit from her father supported by his income tax records and a letter from her father's bank, Mary is able to establish enough financial stability to get the university to issue a Form I-20, and then a student visa.

The story of Yoshi:

Yoshi, from Tokyo, just finished his Bachelors Degree in political science at the University of Tokyo, with an emphasis on international relations. He has been accepted by a major private university in San Francisco, California to study in a doctoral program and speaks pretty good English. The university has established that living expenses for a student are $9,000 per year, and tuition is $15,000 per year, for a total of $24,000. Neither Yoshi nor his family has anywhere near the amount of money necessary to pay for Yoshi's education. Yoshi is able to obtain an F-1 visa, however, by obtaining a letter from the college, establishing that he will be given a full tuition waiver in exchange for teaching one class per semester for the university (see On-Campus Employment, *Chapter Two) and that he will also receive a scholarship to cover his living expenses. Although Yoshi does not have any money, he will not be required to work other than his commitment to work on-campus teaching for the university.*

SPOUSE AND CHILDREN OF F-I

The spouse and dependent children of an F-1 student are entitled to a status known as F-2 (referred to as "derivative" status because it depends on someone else). The family of an F-1 student can apply together with the prospective student for F-2 status, or they may apply at a later time. If the family members are applying separately, the F-1 student is issued a new Form I-20 showing the additional amount of expenses needed to support the dependents. You'll need to supply the Immigration and Naturalization Service (INS) with strong proof of financial resources, because your family members are not entitled to work in the United States in F-2 status.

Be aware that in many developing countries it is very difficult for the wife and children of an F-1 student to obtain F-2 visas, because the U.S. consul often believes that, if the family of the student accompanies the student to the United States, the student has no reason to return home.

TRAVEL IN F-I STATUS

Most individuals in lawful status in the United States may travel to Canada or Mexico for a period of less than 30 days and return to the United States without obtaining a new visa (with the exception of Mexican nationals traveling to Mexico). Traveling students must return to the United States before their lawful status expires. If your visa has expired and you travel to a country other than Canada or Mexico, you must obtain a new visa before applying to enter the United States, even if you are in lawful status.

CHAPTER TWO

Obtaining an F-I Visa for a College or University Student

HOW AND WHERE TO MAKE THE VISA APPLICATION

This Chapter discusses the process for obtaining an F-1 student visa. The process is very similar if you are seeking an M-1 visa (vocational and technical school students) or J-1 visa (exchange visitors), discussed later in this book. Under certain circumstances, citizens of Canada, the Marshall Islands, and Micronesia do not need visas.

To obtain a nonimmigrant visa, you must file an application at one of the embassies or consulates maintained by the U.S. Department of State worldwide. In Taiwan, the application is made at the American Institute.

There are three methods for filing an application for a nonimmigrant visa. You can mail the application to the consulate covering the area of your current or last residence, personally visit the consulate of your current or last residence, or apply at a U.S. consulate in a country other than the country of your current or last residence. The last method is called "third-country processing".

Since a personal interview is not always needed to get a nonimmigrant visa, it's possible to simply mail your visa application with supporting documents, as described below. There is no guarantee, of course, that the application will be approved, and mailed-in applications are often denied. While there is little harm in trying to apply by mail, U.S. consular officers like to have a face to face interviews with someone applying for a visa. That's why in most cases, you'll need to apply for a visa where you are or were last living.

Some consulates, particularly in developing countries, have high refusal rates. That's why some visa applicants try to get a visa using third-country processing. If you are in the United States and have been denied a change of status (see Chapter Three), you may be particularly interested in third-country processing, especially if your last residence was far from the United States. Third country applications are unlikely to be successful, unless you can establish without question that you have a residence abroad, have not abandoned it, and can overcome the presumption of "immigrant intent" (see below). U.S. consular officers discourage "consular shopping" or attempts to find the consulate where an applicant is most likely to be approved. A third-country consular officer is most likely to consider a visa application favorably if you have a legitimate personal or business reason for being in that consular district.

PROVING NONIMMIGRANT INTENT

There is probably no more frustrating problem for the F-1 visa applicant than to be denied because you are unable to convince a consular officer that you honestly intend to obey U.S. immigration laws. Before issuing the visa, the officer must be convinced that you have a residence outside the United States that you have not abandoned and that you have not decided to seek permanent residence in the United States.

Individuals from advanced industrial countries rarely have problems with this issue. If, however, you are from a developing country, have previously violated immigration laws, or have had a permanent immigrant visa petition (see Chapter Ten) filed on your behalf, a consular officer may suspect that, while you enter the United States as a student, you intend to stay permanently.

In cases where nonimmigrant intent is an issue, it is important to show the officer that you have strong ties to your country of residence, such as family, community or social ties, membership in organizations and religious groups, a family business, ownership of property, and bank accounts.

The continuing story of Mary:

Having been accepted at the university, Mary gets all of her papers together and makes an appointment to visit the U.S. consulate in Dublin. The economy in Ireland is very bad, and Mary is concerned that the consular officer will be unwilling to give her a student visa. Coming from a western European country, Mary probably does not have anything to worry about. Should the consul ask her about her plans, she might tell him that, like her father, she plans on studying engineering and that while there is high unemployment for engineers in Ireland, her father has many contacts at the company he works for and is likely to get her a job there. In any event, Mary can explain that she has no family, other than her sister, living in the United States. Her mother, father, brothers, and their families all live in Ireland.

The continuing story of Yoshi:

Yoshi has no close family in either Japan or the United States. Since the experience of the U.S. consular officer who interviews Yoshi is that few people from Japan who come to study in the United States remain unlawfully, Yoshi has no problems in obtaining an F-1 visa and is not questioned at all at the time of his interview.

The story of James:

*James, from Jamaica, is coming to study business adminis-
tration at a top public college in New York City. The tuition is
only $4,000 per year, and James' family has saved enough money
to cover James' living expenses. They have put the money in a
bank account in New York under his name. James' concern is
that most of his family, with the exception of his mother and father,
are in the United States. He has two brothers and two sisters, all
of whom recently became permanent residents. It seems to the consular officer that James' family is shifting its center from Jamaica
to the United States and that James is unlikely to return to the
Jamaica. The consular officer is aware of the high level of unemployment in Jamaica. James has big plans and is able to articu-
late them clearly to the consular officer. His college
studies are the first step of his education. He
intends to obtain a Masters Degree in business
administration. He has worked in the hotel industry in Jamaica as a cashier and assistant book-
keeper, and is planning a career in hotel
management. His parents have not made any
effort to reside in the United States since they just
purchased a retirement home in Jamaica. James
prepares well for his interview at the U.S. consulate, and his F-1 visa is issued to him.*

THE PASSPORT REQUIREMENT

A passport valid for at least six months must be presented at the time of the visa application. It is recommended, however, that the applicant present a passport
which is valid for as long as is allowed in the applicant's
country of citizenship. Under certain circumstances, citizens of Canada, the Marshall Islands, and Micronesia do
not need passports. For an individual unable to obtain a
valid passport, the passport requirement may be waived
but only in exceptional circumstances.

THE VISA APPLICATION

There is little you can do if your nonimmigrant visa application is denied, so it is important that you are courteous and clear in your presentation to the U.S. consular officer. You should make copies of any documents submitted to the consul just in case a problem develops. If your application is denied, the copies will help if the matter is later discussed with an attorney or a foreign student advisor.

Be prepared for certain problems that could arise since there are factors to consider when applying for a nonimmigrant visa. An individual may be "excludable" (ineligible to enter the United States) based on one of the grounds noted in the visa application discussed below or on a ground not specifically discussed in this Handbook. Even if you are found to be excludable for one of these grounds, you may still be able to obtain a nonimmigrant visa, but you will have to apply for a waiver of excludability. If you are concerned that you may be ineligible for a visa, you should speak to an experienced immigration practitioner before applying for a student visa.

The Form I-20, passport, passport-type photograph, proof of financial support, and where necessary, proof of a residence abroad are presented to an U.S. consular officer along with a nonimmigrant visa application, Form OF-156. A copy of this form is reproduced in the appendix on forms.

Among the items of particular importance are:

Item #7
Passport number, date of issuance and date of expiration

See the discussion above about passports. Remember: your passport must be valid for at least six months beyond the date of the visa application.

Item #8
Home Address

A home address abroad, not a temporary address in the United States, should be listed in this space.

Item #20-21
Have you ever applied for an immigrant or nonimmigrant U.S. visa before? Has your U.S. visa ever been canceled?

There is usually no problem if you have received or currently possess a visitor's visa to come to the United States. However, if you have ever been denied a visa or have had one cancelled or voided, the circumstances surrounding the denial and/or the cancellation must be explained at the visa interview. If you have had a prior visa refused or cancelled in this way, be sure to seek the assistance of an experienced immigration attorney before you apply for the F-1 visa.

Item #22
Do you intend to work in the U.S.?

This answer to this question will normally be "no", because as an F-1 student you must show sufficient financial resources to cover the costs and expenses of your education and living expenses without having to work. Where employment is anticipated as part of an academic program, such as a teaching assistantship for a graduate student or an internship for a nursing student, the answer to the question would be a "yes", with a brief explanation why.

Item #24
Who will furnish this financial support, including tickets?

The answer to this question must be supported by full documentation, as described in Chapter One.

Item #29
How long do you plan to stay in the U.S.?

You should answer with the entire period of time that you intend to be in the United States. In other words, if it states on your Form I-20 that it will take you four years to get your Bachelors degree, write four years here.

Item #32(a)
Has anyone ever filed an immigrant visa petition on your behalf? (b) Has labor certification for employment in the U.S. ever been requested by you or on your behalf? (c) Have you or anyone acting for you ever indicated to a U.S. consular or immigration employee a desire to immigrate to the U.S.?

This item is designed to assist the consul in determining whether you have tried in the past to become a permanent resident. If the answer to any of these questions is yes, you may have a difficult time receiving an F-1 visa. If you have previously applied for an immigrant visa, it is hard to show that you intend to return home at the end of your studies. It is not impossible for a person who has applied for an immigrant visa to obtain a student visa, but it is often difficult.

Item #33
Are any of the following in the U.S.? Husband/wife; fiance/fiancee; brother/sister; father/mother; son/daughter?

The presence of a close family relative or fiance in the United States may influence the consular officer to deny the visa application. Many consular officers believe that young single students who travel to the United States for an education will remain here and seek permanent residence. The fact that the prospective student has close family relationships and/or a fiance in the United States may be one factor used by the consular officer to deny the visa, even if other factors, such as finances and foreign residence, are strongly documented.

Item #34
List the countries where you have lived for more than six months during the past five years.

If you have lived in the United States for more than six months during the last five years, especially where you have been out of status, i.e., have overstayed your authorized time, an U.S. consular officer might believe you intend to reside permanently in the United States. In this case, you must provide very strong evidence of your ties to your home country to document your intention to return home after your education in the United States is complete. You should be prepared to explain the reasons for any prolonged stay in the United States in the past five years.

Item #35
Important: All applicants must read and answer the following:

A visa may not be issued to persons who are within specific categories defined by law as inadmissible to the United States (except when a waiver is obtained in advance). Complete information regarding these categories and whether any may be applicable to you can be obtained from this office. Generally, they include persons

- Afflicted with contagious diseases (i.e. tuberculosis) or who have suffered serious mental illness;
- Arrested, convicted for any offense or crime even though subject of a pardon, amnesty, or other such legal action;
- Believed to be narcotic addicts or traffickers;
- Deported from the United States within the last 5 years;
- Who have sought to obtain a visa by misrepresentation or fraud;
- Who are or have been members of certain organizations including Communist organizations and those affiliated therewith;

- Who ordered, incited, assisted or otherwise participated in the persecution of any person because of race, religion, national origin, or political opinion under the control, direct or indirect, of the Nazi Government of Germany, or of the government of any area occupied by, or allied with, the Nazi Government of Germany.

Do any of these appear to apply to you?

If "yes", or if you have any question in this regard, personal appearance at this office is recommended. If it is not possible at this time, attach a statement of facts in your case to this application.

This question is designed to help the consular officer determine whether you are excludable from the United States. If you fall within any of these categories, you probably cannot be issued a nonimmigrant visa, unless you are granted a waiver. A discussion of waivers is beyond the scope of this book. Any applicant who falls within one of the categories listed in Item #35 is strongly advised to seek advice from an experienced immigration practitioner.

OTHER CONCERNS

For some non-English speaking F-1 visa applicants, one area of concern is a knowledge of the English language. If the Form I-20 does not indicate any arrangements for studying English, the consul will sometimes check your English proficiency. Since many schools require the Test of English as a Foreign Language or "TOEFL" (see Chapter One) as part of the application process, this informal test should not be a problem. You may be asked to read either a newspaper or other written English language material out loud to the consul and then may be asked to explain the meaning in your own words. You may be asked to read the Form I-20 or parts of it out loud to the consul and asked to explain what it means in your own words.

An applicant with marginal proficiency in English might be referred for more formal testing by the consular officer. If you intend to study English in the United States, the consul should be shown the arrangements you have made for your English studies.

Another area of concern is a lack of obvious purpose for the proposed education or training. The U.S. consul might be inclined to deny the issuance of an F-1 student visa if you present an I-20 Form for a course of study that appears to have no application in your home country. If you are concerned about this issue, you should prepare a convincing explanation for the visa interview as to why such an education would be useful either in your home country or in another country abroad. Unless you can establish that employment opportunities are available outside the United States, your serious intent to leave the United States upon completion of your studies would be in question. You might wish to support your explanation with an offer of employment for a date to begin after the completion of your studies or with other written documentation.

PHOTOGRAPHS AND FEE

In order to obtain a student visa, you must present, in addition to the documents discussed above, a passport type photograph. Check with the consulate to determine whether a fee is also required.

CHECKLIST OF DOCUMENTATION REQUIRED FOR AN F-I VISA APPLICATION.

a. Form I-20 fully completed in the original and signed by an official of the school;

b. A valid passport with an expiration date at least six months in the future;

c. Form OF-156, the visa application form;

    d. Two photographs;

    e. Evidence of financial support and ties to home country;

    f. Fee, if any.

WHAT HAPPENS WHEN YOUR APPLICATION FOR A VISA IS GRANTED?

If your application is approved, a nonimmigrant visa will be stamped into your passport. The stamp will include the date the stamp was issued, the period of validity, whether it is a single or multiple entry visa, your name, the place where the visa is issued, and the name of the school to which you are destined.

The "validity" of a visa refers to the time for which this particular visa is useful for entry into the United States. It may be the same or different from the amount of time you actually intend to spend in the United States. For instance, an individual intending to study in the United States at a four year college may obtain a visa that is valid for three months. In this situation, that means you have three months to use that visa to enter the United States. Once you apply for entry at a U.S. port, the admitting immigration officer will usually admit you for the duration of your intended stay in the United States. In this case, for an F-1 attending a college or university, the officer will note "d\s" or "duration of status". (See "Duration of Status" in Chapter Four.)

If a student fails to use the visa within the three month period, it will no longer be valid. But once you use the visa to enter the United States, you should be allowed to remain as long as you maintain status.

The number of entries — one, two, or multiple — refers to the number of times the visa can be used to enter the United States before the visa expires. A single entry visa means that you can use that visa only once. If you are a student with a single entry visa and you subsequently travel to another country (other than a trip of 30 days or less to Canada or Mexico), you will have to obtain a new visa to enter the United States, even if you have been maintaining your status and was granted duration of status at the time of entry (see Chapter One for more on travel while in the United States in student status). If you have a multiple entry visa, you will be able to come in and out of the United States as you like, provided you maintain your status and carry with you proof of your student status in the form of an I-20 ID Form endorsed by your foreign student advisor.

ENTRY INTO THE UNITED STATES

When, as a international student, you apply to enter the United States (unless you are exempt from the visa requirement), you must present a visa issued to you by an U.S. consular officer abroad. The Immigration and Naturalization (INS) officer at the port of entry (who is called an Immigration Inspector) will look at the visa, your passport, and Form I-20. The purpose of the inspection is to determine your eligibility for admission into the United States as a nonimmigrant student. The Inspector has the same right as a consular officer to question you as to your financial status, your intentions regarding working in the United States, and your intent to attend the school indicated on the Form I-20. If you pass the inspection, you are given Form I-94 (Arrival/Departure Record) which is noted to indicate you have been admitted to the United States. If you are an F-1 student, you will be admitted for duration of status.

VISA DENIALS

If an application for nonimmigrant visa is denied, in most cases, you will be told the reasons for the denial and should receive written notice of those reasons. Sometimes you can ask the visa officer to reconsider the denial. For instance, if the application was denied because you failed to show sufficient financial resources, you may be able to return to the consul with additional financial information establishing your ability to finance your education. If, however, the consular officer insists on denying the application, it is very difficult to get that consular officer's decision overturned.

Besides a request for reconsideration, you may seek an advisory opinion from the Department of State asking them to reverse the decision of the consular officer. Where the officer's decision is based on an issue of fact (such as when the officer believes you do not intend to return to your country at the completion of your studies), it is almost impossible to get an advisory opinion at the Department of State reversing the consular officer's decision. Where an issue of law is involved, such as an interpretation of government regulations or statutes, the Department of State will sometimes contradict the consul officer's decision. An individual seeking an advisory opinion may write to: Advisory Opinions Division for Visa Services, United States Department of State, 2401 E Street, N.W., Washington, D.C. 20522-0113. You may also want to consider the assistance of an experienced immigration attorney.

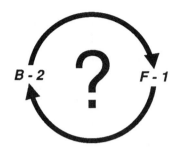

CHAPTER THREE

Changing Status While in the United States

If you are already in the United States in another non-immigrant classification, such as a B-2 visitor for pleasure, you can apply to have your immigration status changed to F-1 student. In some instances, your foreign student advisor will assist in preparing the application.

You should be aware though that it is sometimes difficult for a B-2 visitor to change to F-1 student status. The U.S. Immigration and Naturalization Service (INS) tends to think that you might be trying to avoid the possible difficulties of applying at the U.S. consulate in your home country. It is always wise for an F-1 student to include with the application for change of status an explanation, in the form of an affidavit (see Glossary), as to why the change is sought and why no visa application was made in your home country. The affidavit should also explain the reason you want to study here. It is often helpful to explain that your desire to study in the United States was formed after arrival, if that is the case. You may also find it useful to explain what you intend to do with your U.S. education when you return to your country.

It is important that you are "in status", that is, that your authorized period of stay must not have expired at the time the change of status application is filed with INS. If you are "out of status", you must have a very good reason why your status has lapsed.

The Application to Change Nonimmigrant Status, Form I-539, with supporting documentation, is filed with the INS office having jurisdiction over where you are living while you are here. A copy of the application and all attachments should be made before filing. You should keep a copy in case the INS loses the original paperwork. You should also keep the INS filing receipt as well as the canceled check and/or money order receipt. While the INS does not regularly lose applications, if the application is misplaced, proof of filing will be very important.

In addition to Form I-539 (discussed below), your Form I-94 (the arrival/departure document issued to a nonimmigrant entering the United States), Form I-20, and supporting documentation regarding your ability to pay for your education (as discussed in detail in Chapter One) must be included in the application.

Sometimes a prospective F-1 student outside the United States is able to obtain a B-2 visitor's visa for the purpose of visiting or applying for admission to a college or university. If the B-2 visa is issued for this purpose, the consul will note "prospective student" below the visa. Submitting a copy of this page from your passport will facilitate the granting of a change of status application.

The story of Harry:

Harry, from Hong Kong, graduated high school and came to visit his aunt and uncle in the United States, staying with them in their lovely new home in San Diego. He spends the summer enjoying life on the beach, practices his English with the other young men and women in the area, and enjoys life in anticipation of a gruelling four years at the university back home. Harry likes San Diego so much that when one of his friends suggests that he speak

to a foreign student advisor at the state university, Harry agrees and learns that they have a special admission program for students who will study English as a second language for one year and then enter a regular four year college program. Harry is very excited about the university's program and, with the assistance of the school's foreign student advisor, applies for a change of status. He explains in a sworn statement that when he came to the United States he had no intention of studying here, that he had been accepted into a university in Hong Kong (he submits a copy of his acceptance letter as proof), and that he only learned of the availability of the program in San Diego after he had arrived. Harry's application for change of status is approved. His Form I-94 which he received when he entered the United States as a B-2 visitor is marked C/S F-1 D/S. ("C/S" means change of status, and "D/S" refers to duration of status.) Harry can now remain in the United States as long as he maintains his status as a student. If Harry wants to go home for a visit or vacation in Europe, he will have to obtain a new Form I-20 and apply abroad for an F-1 visa in order to reenter the United States.

The story of Nick:

Nick, from Nigeria, applied for a change of status from B-2 visitor to F-1 student one week after he arrived in New York City. He submitted the application for change of status with no documentation and, though his brother did exactly the same thing the month before and his brother's application was approved, sadly, Nick's was denied. The letter denying the application states that Nick must leave the United States in 30 days or else deportation proceedings may be instituted against him. While Nick has sufficient funds to attend college and live in New York City without working, a trip back to Nigeria to obtain an F-1 visa would be very costly and seriously interfere with his studies. With the help of the school's foreign student advisor, Nick requests that the INS reconsider the denial of his application. Nick explains that he did not deceive the U.S. consular officer when he applied for the visitor's visa to the United States. In fact, Nick had explained that he was hoping that he would be able to get into a college or university and had discussed the possibility with an admissions officer but wanted to visit New York and the university first before making a final decision. He had presented the consular officer with a letter from the university inviting him to visit the campus. The consular officer had written "prospective student" under the B-2 visitor's visa he had issued to Nick but Nick had neglected to include a copy of the visa when he submitted his application for change of status. Nick's motion to reconsider is granted and he receives in the mail his Form I-94 with a change of status to F-1 noted.

COMPLETING THE APPLICATION FOR CHANGE OF STATUS

Several items on Form I-539, a copy of which is reproduced in the appendix, need special attention:

Part 4 - Additional Information
For applicant -

I. Provide passport information

INS regulations require that a passport be valid for at least six months after the time of filing of this application. Usually the change of status application will be granted even when the passport is valid for less than six months.

3a. Are you, or any other person included in this application, an applicant for an immigrant visa or adjustment of status to permanent residence?

3b. Has an immigrant petition ever been filed for you, or for any other person included in this application?

If, as an applicant for a change of status, you have previously filed for lawful permanent residence, or have had a petition filed on your behalf, you may face a difficult time in obtaining a change of status. The INS requires that you have an intention to return to your own home country after completing your studies. An application for permanent residence indicates, to the contrary, an intention to remain in the United States permanently. If this is the case, you should seek the advice of an experienced immigration practitioner before filing for a change of status.

3c. Have you, or any other person included in this application, ever been arrested or convicted of any criminal offense since last entry the U.S.?

A person who has engaged in unlawful activity may be denied a change of status or may be deportable from the United States. If the answer to this question is yes, you should speak to an experienced immigration practitioner before submitting the application.

3d. Have you, or any other person included in this application done anything which violated the terms of the nonimmigrant status you now hold?

A yes answer to this question in most cases will result in the denial of your application unless there is a satisfactory explanation for having violated status. You should consult with an experienced immigration practitioner before submitting the application if the answer to this question is yes.

3e. Are you or any other person included in this application, now in exclusion or deportation proceedings?

A person in exclusion or deportation proceedings is extremely unlikely to be granted a change of nonimmigrant status. A person who is served with notice of pending exclusion or deportation proceedings should consult an experienced immigration practitioner immediately.

**3f. Have you, or any other person included in this applica-
tion, been employed in the U.S. since last admitted or
granted an extension or change of status?**

Some nonimmigrants, including students, may work.
(See Chapters Five and Eight.) Some may not. An individual in B-2 visitor status, in most cases, is not eligible for
employment in the United States. If the answer to this
question is yes, and you are not 100% sure that employment was properly authorized, you should speak to an
experienced immigration practitioner before submitting
this application.

THE CHANGE OF STATUS APPROVAL PROCESS

If the application for change of status is approved, the
INS will return your copy of Form I-20 stamped or marked
"D/S" or "d/s", usually in the upper right-hand corner of
the page. This means that you can remain in the United
States in F-1 status for the duration of status or the period
of time stated at Item 5 of the I-20 Form, plus practical
training (see Chapter Five), if any, plus an additional sixty
days. The I-94 Form will be stamped on the back to
reflect the change of status.

If you do not hear from the INS about your application
for change of nonimmigrant status prior to the expiration of
your authorized stay, you don't have to leave the United
States when your stay expires. Similarly, nothing in INS
regulations prevents a college or university from allowing
you to begin classes while your application for change of status is pending. An individual whose application for change
of status was timely filed but has not heard from the INS
may be considered by some INS officials as a deportable
alien. In most cases, however, you will not be asked by the
INS to leave unless and until the application is denied.

Students and their advisors become understandably
concerned by the long delays that often accompany an
application for change of nonimmigrant status. The pro-

cessing time for the application will normally be from a few weeks to six months or longer depending on the workload and resources available at the District Office of the INS where the application is filed. (A list of the District Offices of the INS and the cities they are responsible for can be found in the appendix.) A foreign student advisor can usually advise the student about local processing times.

If your application has been pending longer than is usual, a foreign student advisor may have a contact at the INS office they can call to check on the status of your application. If not, you can write to the INS yourself, making sure to send the letter certified/return receipt requested (see "Mail" in Chapter Fifteen). If all else fails you or your advisor might consider contacting the congressional representative who represents the district where the school is located or where you live. Even though you are not a U.S. citizen, the elected representatives who serve the area can often help with immigration and other problems. To find out the name of the U.S. Representative or the U.S. Senators for the district you live in, call the local office of the League of Women Voters, a public library, or directory assistance.

Once the application for change of status to F-1 has been granted, you can remain in that status in the United States as long as you pursue a full course of study. As an F-1 student, should you leave the country at any time during the course of studies, you must go to an U.S. consular office abroad to apply for an F-1 visa in order to return to the United States in F-1 status.

WHAT IF THE APPLICATION FOR CHANGE OF STATUS IS DENIED?

If your application for change of status is denied, the INS will return the I-94 Form to you with a letter of denial. INS usually requests that you leave the United States on or before a fixed date. While the denial letter may indicate that failure to depart may or will result in deportation proceedings being instituted, that is often not the case. While there is no appeal from the denial of the application for change of status, you can request the INS to reconsider or review the denial. If your application for change of status to F-1 has been denied, you should seek advice from your foreign student advisor or an experienced immigration practitioner.

Checklist for a change of status to F-1 student:

a. **Form I-539.** This is the application for change of nonimmigrant status.

b. **Form I-20.** This is the form issued by the school's admission office or foreign student advisor after acceptance by the school. It must be an original form, filled out completely and bearing an original signature of the international student advisor or other designated school official and the student.

c. **Original Form I-94.** This is the arrival document stapled into the passport at the time of entry into the United States.

d. **Fee of $70.00, personal check or money order recommended, payable to the INS.** A canceled check or money order receipt with the applicant's name and Form I-539 written on it will provide proof of filing of the application should the application be lost at the INS office. BE CAREFUL: Fees change, so be sure to pay the correct amount.

e. Evidence of Financial Support

f. Supporting affidavit

CHAPTER FOUR

Maintaining F-1 Student Status

As a student, you must comply with all the conditions of your status. This includes pursuing a full course of study, notifying the Immigration and Naturalization Service (INS) when changing certain educational objectives, attending the school designated on the I-20 Form, not working without authorization, and leaving the United States after completing your studies (unless you change to another nonimmigrant status or become a permanent resident). If you fail to maintain status, you may be considered deportable by the INS. Although very few students are deported for being out of status, violating immigration laws may make you ineligible for various benefits, including authorization to work.

PURSUING A FULL COURSE OF STUDY

The number of credits that constitute a full course of study varies from institution to institution. A foreign student advisor or "FSA" may allow you to engage in less than a full course of study due to initial English language difficulties, unfamiliarity with U.S. teaching methods, health problems, or improper course level placement. An F-1 student with an authorized course load is considered to be maintaining status.

CHANGES IN EDUCATIONAL PROGRAM

A foreign student may change a major field of study within the same educational program while maintaining F-1 student status. For example, you can change your major from physics to English without a problem. In contrast, movement from one educational level to another, such as from a Bachelors degree program to a Masters program, requires that you notify the INS within 15 days of the beginning of the new semester. When you change levels, your foreign student advisor will prepare a new I-20 Form, the first page of which will be submitted to the INS. The second page, the Form I-20 ID, will be given to you to keep.

TRANSFER OF SCHOOLS

To maintain lawful F-1 student status, you must attend the school or college listed on the Form I-20 to which you were admitted. To change schools, you must follow specific INS procedures.

To transfer between schools, as an F-1 student you must first have pursued a full course of study at the school you were authorized to attend on Form I-20. You should notify the school for which you were admitted to the United States of the desire to transfer, since the foreign student advisor at the new school will seek information from the old school regarding your maintenance of status. You should notify the foreign student advisor at the new school within 15 days of your enrollment. After the transfer, the foreign student advisor at the new school will then submit page one of a new Form I-20 with the notation "transfer completed on (date)" to the INS. The foreign student advisor will give the second page, the Form I-20 ID, to you.

If you have never registered, attended, or pursued a full course of study at the school you were admitted to attend in the United States, you have not maintained lawful F-1 status and must apply for reinstatement to student status before being considered a lawful F-1 student at a new school. Most schools will allow a student whose application for reinstatement is pending to attend classes, but you will be ineligible for benefits incident to F-1 status (such as on-campus employment, see Chapter Five) until the application for reinstatement is approved.

DURATION OF STATUS

As an F-1 student, you are authorized to be in the United States for a period known as "duration of status" (marked "D/S" or "d/s" on you visa). This period includes the time a student is pursuing a full course of study in the educational program, plus any periods of authorized practical training (see Chapter Five), plus 60 days. You must then depart from the United States unless you change to another nonimmigrant status or become a permanent resident of this country.

EXTENSION OF STAY

As an F-1 student, you don't have to apply for an extension of stay as long as you maintain status and make normal progress toward a complete educational objective as indicated on your Form I-20.

If you can't meet the expected completion date, you must apply to your foreign student advisor for a program extension in the 30 day period before that day arrives. The foreign student advisor will certify Form I-538 (application for school transfer) if you (a) have continually maintained status and (b) the delay preventing you from completing the full course of study in a timely matter was caused by a compelling academic or medical reason. Acceptable reasons include a change of major or a change of research topic, an unexpected research problem, or documented illnesses. Academic probation or suspension is not considered a compelling reason. The foreign student advisor will issue a new Form I-20 showing a new program completion date. The I-538 Form and page one of the new Form I-20 will be forwarded to the INS for notification. The advisor will give you the I-20 ID student copy.

REINSTATEMENT TO STUDENT STATUS

Any F-1 student who fails to maintain proper F-1 non-immigrant student status may return to F-1 status by one of two ways, depending on the circumstances:

1. applying for reinstatement to student status, or

2. leaving the United States and reentering with a student visa and Form I-20.

Examples of failure to maintain status are:

1. using a Form I-20 from one school to obtain a visa or enter the United States but at the last minute decide to attend another;

2. failing to complete a full course of study in a timely manner but the reason is not a compelling academic or medical one, or;

3. transfering schools without following the proper procedure.

If you find yourself in this situation and wish to seek reinstatement to student status, you should speak to your foreign student advisor who will assist you in applying to the INS District Office having jurisdiction over where you live. A request for reinstatement to student status is made on Form I-539, Application to Extend/Change Nonimmigrant Status. Form I-20 and any supporting documentation explaining why you failed to maintain status should be attached.

You must be able to show that you violated the terms of F-1 nonimmigrant status unwillingly or by circumstances beyond your control or, in rare cases, that a failure to reinstate you to lawful F-1 status will result in your suffering extreme hardship. You must be pursuing or intend to pursue a full course of study at the school which issues the current Form I-20. You must not be deportable on any grounds (except failure to maintain status), and you must not have engaged in unauthorized employment.

It is often helpful for you to submit a letter to the INS explaining the circumstances why you failed to maintain your student status.

The continuing story of Mary:

Mary, now in the United States studying engineering, found that subject not to her taste. She became fascinated with the U.S. political system and decided instead to major in political science. The college she was attending was primarily focused on the physical sciences not the social sciences, so Mary decided to change schools and was accepted into another institution in another city. She spent only one semester at the school of engineering and began her second semester at the school of political science at the very last minute.

When Mary learned that she would be able to attend the second school on short notice, she went to see her foreign student advisor but it was the Christmas holidays and the office was closed. She moved to the new city

and school and began classes. The foreign student advisor at Mary's new school kept asking her to obtain proof that she was a full-time student and had maintained her status at her first school. Mary was so busy with her classes that it was not until the semester was almost over that Mary finally obtained the necessary information from the school she first attended. The information reflected that, in fact, Mary had attended classes and engaged in a full course of study and had successfully completed her first semester. However, since she did not obtain the information sooner, Mary's foreign student advisor was not able to make a timely notification to the INS and Mary is considered out of status. However, she may apply for reinstatement of status by explaining that her decision to change schools was made at the last minute. She should emphasize her changing educational interest and its potential uses to her when she returns to Ireland.

The continuing story of James:

James never attended the school he had planned to go to when he left Jamaica. Upon arriving to the United States, he visited the college and found many of the courses he intended to take his first year were filled and that others had been eliminated due to budget cuts. He was able to gain admission to another college in the same city, and although he had not even begun classes at his first college, he was allowed by the administration at the new school to begin classes immediately. Since he never attended the first school, he cannot apply for a transfer of schools but rather must apply for reinstatement of status. Since his reason for changing was beyond his control, he should be successful. He must submit Form I-539, Application to Extend/Change Nonimmigrant Status, with Form I-20 from the new school as well.

**CHECKLIST FOR REINSTATEMENT TO
STUDENT STATUS:**

a. Form I-539, Application to Extend/Change
    Nonimmigrant Status;

b. Filing fee of $70.00 (but remember to double
    check the fee to be sure it has not changed);

c. A new Form I-20;

d. A financial statement; and

e. A letter and supporting documentation as to the
    reason reinstatement is justified.

If you are unsuccessful in applying for reinstatement
of status, you can still return to the United States following
travel abroad, provided you have a valid multiple entry
student visa. You must bring with you a new Form I-20
issued by your foreign student advisor. Students whose F-
1 visa is no longer valid for entry into the United States
will need to apply for a new visa at an U.S. consulate.

CHAPTER FIVE

Working While Studying for the F-1 Student

As a prospective F-1 student, you must establish that you will not need to work illegally while studying. However, many foreign students wish to work to gain experience, interact with U.S. business, or supplement family support or personal resources due to changed financial need. In this Chapter, we will discuss pre- and post-graduate student employment eligibility requirements and restrictions for F-1 students.

ON-CAMPUS EMPLOYMENT

On-campus employment by F-1 students is permitted as long as the student works no more than 20 hours a week while school is in session. Students may be employed full-time during vacations and recess periods, so long as they intend to register for the next term.

On-campus employment means employment performed on the premises of the school or at an affiliated off-site location. It may mean employment on the campus of a school of a type normally performed by students (such as work in the school library, cafeteria, or student store), or employment which is part of a student's scholarship, fellowship or assistantship. In the case of off-campus locations, the place of employment must be associated or educationally affiliated with the school's established curriculum, or related to contractually funded research projects at the post-graduate level.

In general, on-campus employers know that as an F-1 student you hold a valid Form I-20 that allows you to work up to 20 hours a week. You may need a letter from your foreign student advisor which explains that you are authorized to work on-campus. The authorization letter from the foreign student advisor will also be helpful in assisting you to obtain a social security card. Students who accept on-campus employment are exempt from having to obtain an employment authorization card (EAD) from the Immigration and Naturalization Service (INS).

OFF-CAMPUS CO-OP PROGRAMS AND INTERNSHIPS

Cooperative training or "co-op" programs and internships are generally referred to by the INS as "curricular practical training". Some schools have co-op programs, internships or work study programs as part of their regular curriculum, and you may be required to participate in a work study program as part of a degree requirement or regular course of study. However, you cannot qualify for curricular practical training until you have been enrolled in the school for at least nine months, although if you are enrolled in graduate studies that require immediate participation in curricular practical training you can begin immediately.

If the curricular practical training is twelve months (on a full-time basis) in length, the time you spend in curricular practical training will make you ineligible for post-completion practical training.

To receive permission to engage in curricular practical training, you must apply to your foreign student advisor. You do not need INS approval of the curricular practical training, but you must have your Form I-20 ID endorsed by your foreign student advisor before beginning practical training. The application consists of Form I-538, Certification by Designated School Official, and Form I-20.

The foreign student advisor will endorse your Form I-20 ID "full-time (or part-time) curricular practical training authorized from (date) to (date)" and sign and date Form I-20 ID before returning it to you. You may then begin curricular practical training, but only after receiving the Form I-20 ID endorsed by the foreign student advisor.

PRE-COMPLETION PRACTICAL TRAINING

Off-campus pre-completion practical training in a field related to your studies is permitted for F-1 students so long as you work no more than 20 hours a week while school is in session. You may be employed full-time during vacations and recess periods so long as you intend to register for the next term. Time spent in pre-completion practical training will be deducted from the twelve months full-time employment available for post-completion practical training.

For example, if you work 20 hours per week for six months, you would have three months deducted from the twelve months allowed you for post-completion practical training.

Permission to engage in pre-completion practical training requires only that your foreign student advisor certify, by signing Form I-538, that the employment is directly related to your major area of study and commensurate with your educational level. The foreign student advisor will endorse Form I-20 ID to show that the practical training is to begin and end on a certain date and whether it is for part-time or full-time employment. Form I-20 ID will be returned to you, and Form I-538 will be submitted to the INS.

Once you get the endorsed Form I-20 ID from the foreign student advisor, you must apply in person at the INS office having jurisdiction over your residence for an EAD by submitting Form I-765 (application for employment authorization) and the proper fee.

EMPLOYMENT AUTHORIZATION BASED ON SEVERE ECONOMIC HARDSHIP

Where unforeseen circumstances lead to a change in your economic situation, you can obtain permission to work off-campus in any job of your choosing, 20 hours per week, full-time during vacation periods. Perhaps you lost your financial aid or on-campus employment through no fault of your own, your cost of living or tuition unexpectedly increased, you have incurred large medical expenses, the value of currency from your country has decreased, or your sponsor has suffered an economic loss. Employment based on economic necessity is not deducted from time allowed for post-completion practical training, but you must have completed one academic year in F-1 status to qualify and be in good academic standing.

If you are seeking economic hardship employment authorization, you must obtain Form I-538 from your foreign student advisor who will certify that neither "pilot program" (see below) nor on-campus employment is available or sufficient to meet your unexpected economic need. Form I-538 is submitted with Form I-765 and the fee to the INS office in the district where you live. You should include with your application an affidavit (see Glossary) with supporting documents explaining the basis for your claim of economic hardship.

The continuing story of Yoshi:

After Yoshi's first year of graduate studies, an economic crisis at the University he was attending resulted in a partial loss of his scholarship. His on-campus teaching position which had allowed him to afford to attend the school, was also cut back. He obtained a letter from the financial aid officer at the university establishing this loss of support, a letter from the Dean of

Faculty as to the loss of part of his teaching income, and together with an affidavit regarding his financial situation and Form I-538 certified by his foreign student advisor, he filed Form I-765 with the INS. He was granted employment authorization to work part-time off-campus, and obtained a part-time job as an international commodities trader.

OTHER PRE-COMPLETION OFF-CAMPUS EMPLOYMENT: PILOT OFF-CAMPUS EMPLOYMENT PROGRAM

After completing one academic year in F-1 status, you can work off-campus for an employer of your choosing if the employer provides the school and the Department of Labor with an attestation that (1) the employer recruited for the position for at least 60 days and (2) your wages will be comparable to those paid to domestic workers. The employment need not be related to your field of study. This is known as the "Pilot Off-Campus Employment Program". To qualify, you must be in status and in good academic standing as determined by your foreign student advisor. Permission to accept off-campus employment is limited to no more than 20 hours a week when school is in session and full-time only when school is not in session.

The difficult aspect of obtaining "pilot program" off-campus employment is convincing an employer to comply with and submit the labor attestation. A prospective employer should recognize that it must recruit for 60 days, but need not advertise in a newspaper. Placing a notice with the state's department of labor and posting a notice at the job site is sufficient.

A foreign student advisor may authorize off-campus employment in one year intervals with renewals possible during the validity of an attestation. If you transfer to a new school, your new foreign student advisor can renew any off-campus employment authorization if you present the advisor with a copy of the original attestation or new attestation. If this is not done, the employment authorization is considered terminated.

You must complete Form I-538, Certification by Designated School Official, have it certified by your foreign student advisor, and then submit it to the INS. Off-campus employment authorized by a foreign student advisor is employer specific. This means that you need not obtain an EAD from the INS.

The continuing story of James:

James wants to work while studying. His program in hotel management does not require work experience as a condition to receiving a degree nor does his program allow him to earn academic credit for gaining related work experience, so he is not eligible for curricular practical training. He has found a shoe store willing to employ him as a clerk 10 to 20 hours per week. The shoe store posted a notice of the job position availability at the personnel office of the company and notified the local state employment agency who listed the job for sixty days. Since the job was only part-time and the hours varied so much no U.S. workers applied. The employer filed a labor attestation with the Department of Labor and sent a copy to the foreign student advisor at James' college. Now the foreign student advisor can authorize James to work at the shoe store.

POST-COMPLETION PRACTICAL TRAINING

F-1 students are entitled to up to one year of post-completion practical training. However, as explained above, if you have received one year or more of full-time curricular practical training, you are ineligible for practical training after the completion of your studies. Note also that time spent in pre-completion practical training is deducted from the twelve month maximum. Practical training can be authorized after the completion of all coursework requirements for a degree.

Authorization for post-completion practical training will be granted for a maximum of twelve months and takes effect only after you have completed your course of study. In any event, you must complete your practical training within a fourteen month period following the completion of your studies. An F-1 student may be authorized to engage in post-completion practical training only once for the duration of student status, regardless of the number of degrees pursued. For example, if you get a Bachelors degree and thereafter receive twelve months practical training, and you then decide to pursue a Masters degree, practical training would not be available upon completion of your Masters program.

You can submit your request to engage in post-completion practical training from 120 days before up to 60 days after the completion of your course of study. This request to accept practical training is made to the foreign student advisor at your school. You must make the request for post-completion practical training on Form I-538 accompanied by your current Form I-20 ID.

Post-completion practical training is intended to give you an opportunity to round off your academic studies. The foreign student advisor need certify only that the employment is appropriate for your educational level and is directly related to your major area of study. This certification is accomplished by your foreign student advisor signing Form I-538.

Your foreign student advisor will also endorse Form I-20 ID to show that the practical training is recommended to begin on a certain date. Form I-20 ID will be returned to you for further processing and Form I-538 will be submitted to the INS.

Once you receive the endorsed Form I-20 ID from your foreign student advisor, you must apply in person at the INS office having jurisdiction over your residence for an EAD, during this same 120 day period of time, i.e., within 90 days before the completion of study and 30 days after completion. As an F-1 student seeking practical training, you may not accept employment until you have been issued the EAD. The application for the EAD is made on

Form I-765. The application for employment authorization is made at the INS office and must include completed Form I-765 with a filing of fee and Form I-20 ID (and in some INS Districts a copy of the form) endorsed by your foreign student advisor.

The INS will make a decision on the Form I-765 and issue you an EAD on the basis of recommendation made by your Foreign Student Advisor. If for some reason the District Director denies the application made on Form I-765, that denial may not be appealed, but a request to reconsider based on new or additional documentation can be submitted to the INS. The application process for the EAD requires a personal appearance.

An F-1 student, who has an unexpired EAD issued for post-completion practical training and returns from a temporary trip abroad and who is otherwise admissible, may resume employment. You must present the EAD and Form I-20 ID when entering the United States. Form I-20 ID must have been endorsed for reentry by your foreign student advisor within the last six months.

The continuing story of Mary:

Mary successfully completed her studies for a Bachelor's degree in political science. She obtained permission to engage in postgraduate practical training and applied for an EAD which she received from the INS. She had no offer of employment when she received the EAD, but the EAD was valid for 14 months and it took six months for Mary to find a job teaching U.S. history at a community college. While her studies were in political science, teaching U.S. history is close enough to her area of study to qualify as practical training. Mary can teach for eight months (fourteen months minus six months) in F-1 status as a practical trainee. If she wants to continue to work beyond those eight months, she will have to change to another status such as H-1B temporary worker (see Chapter Eight*) or permanent resident (see* Chapter Ten*).*

CHAPTER SIX

M-1 Status for Vocational and Technical School Students

International students may obtain M-1 status to attend schools offering technical or vocational education. Programs include such subjects as auto mechanics, paralegal studies, secretarial skills, beauty and cosmetics, keyboard operation, and computer programming, among others.

With some important exceptions discussed below, the process for obtaining M-1 status (either through consular processing or a change of status) and the rules regarding maintenance of status are similar to those that apply to F-1 college or university students. Prospective or current M-1 students should read Chapters One through Five carefully.

In general, prospective M-1 students should follow the procedures outlined for F-1 students, noting the differences discussed below. Note particularly that the rules regarding employment of M-1 are very different to those which apply to F-1 students.

You should also note that M-1 students may not change to F-1 status and can only change to H-1B status (see Chapter Eight) if the qualifying education was not acquired through M-1 status. An M-1 student who wants to become an F-1 student would have to leave the country and apply for an F-1 visa at a U.S. consulate.

CONSULAR PROCESSING

If you decide to seek M-1 student status, you should be aware that consular officers look at the use to which you intend to put your proposed training as a significant factor in granting an M-1 visa. In other words, if you can't use the vocational education or training from your proposed M-1 study in your home country, the visa may not be granted. Unless you can establish that there are employment opportunities available in your own country, the consul will question whether you seriously intend to leave the United States at the end of your M-1 student status.

At the interview for the M-1 visa, you must prove your ability to pay all tuition and living costs for the entire period of your proposed stay. The consular officer may also require you to produce a prepaid round trip ticket to and from the United States.

The story of Gerard:

Gerard, from France, would like to study film editing in the United States. There is a university in Los Angeles which is famous for its film program, but Gerard has neither the resources nor the desire to obtain a degree in this subject. He would like to develop the skills without taking the other courses that would be normally required in a Bachelors degree program such as English, mathematics, and history. The university, in addition to its

Bachelors and Masters degree program in film, also has a continuing education program which does not provide a degree but offers a certificate. The program involves full-time study for one year.

While there are certainly film editing programs in France, the California program is considered to be unique. Gerard has been working in the film industry in France and obtains a letter from his current employer indicating that a position will await him upon completion of the one year course. He obtains Form I-20 from the school and is able to establish sufficient resources to pay for his education and living expenses without working in the United States. He is granted an M-1 visa.

CHANGING TO M-1 STATUS WHILE IN THE UNITED STATES

You can apply for a change from a nonimmigrant status to M-1 status without leaving the country. The major difference from F-1 change of status processing is that the M-1 student is not allowed a B-2 "prospective student" visa to enter the United States. Generally, as an applicant for a change of status to M-1, you must be even more diligent than the F-1 applicant in explaining why you did not apply for an M-1 visa prior to coming here.

The story of Pilar:

Pilar, from Argentina, has a Bachelors degree in Spanish literature with an emphasis on the renowned Spanish writer Cervantes. Pilar is frustrated because she is unable to find a job, but decides to take advantage of her unemployed status to visit her girlfriend, Catherine, in California. While in California, she learns of a vocational school in computer programming. Her friend Catherine is a computer programmer and enjoys the work and makes a decent income. Pilar knows that despite a weak economy in her country, computer programmers, especially those trained in the United States on the latest U.S. equipment, are in great demand in Argentina. She applies to the school, is accepted, and obtains Form I-20 from the school's admissions office.

When she applies for a change of nonimmigrant status from B-2 visitor to M-1 student, she submits, in addition to her Form

I-20 and proof that she can support herself without working, the following documents: an affidavit from herself explaining her job possibilities in her country of Argentina; her activities in the three months since she entered the United States indicating that she has not worked and that she has travelled extensively throughout California; an explanation of how she learned about the computer programming course; an affidavit from her friend confirming Pilar's story regarding her visit to the United States and her activities here; and a letter her father helps her obtain from a company in Argentina offering Pilar employment when she completes her studies. The letter from the potential employer in Argentina contained a job description and an explanation of the link between the education Pilar will receive in the United States and the job duties in Argentina.

MAINTENANCE OF STATUS FOR M-I STUDENTS

M-1 students must pursue a full course of study and attend the school designated on the Form I-20 they used to obtain student status, unless they apply to transfer schools. They may not work without authorization and must depart the United States within 30 days of completion of their studies, unless they change to another nonimmigrant status or become permanent residents.

Unlike an F-1 student, as an M-1 student you are not admitted for "duration of status". You can be admitted for no more than one year even if the program you intend to enroll in requires longer to complete. If you wish to continue your studies in the United States, and many programs for which M-1 students come into the United States last more than one year, you must apply for an extension of stay. Assuming your extension is approved, you will be granted sufficient time to complete your studies plus 30 days to depart the United States. In order to obtain an extension of stay, you must file Form I-539 requesting an extension, no more than 60 days and no less than 15 days prior to the end of your first period of study. As a practical matter, an application which is filed anytime before the first period of stay expires, will be considered the same as those filed 15 days before. A timely filed application for extension will allow you to remain in the United States until the application is decided by the Immigration and Naturalization Service (INS), and you are not considered out of status while that decision is being made.

It is more difficult for M-1 students to transfer schools than for F-1 students. Immigration regulations state that an M-1 student cannot transfer to another school after six months after your first admission to the United States (as an M-1 student) unless you are forced to do so due to circumstances beyond your control. M-1 students cannot change their educational objectives as F-1 students are allowed to do.

Another important difference between F-1 and M-1 students is the manner in which you must apply to transfer schools. For the F-1 student, the INS merely needs to be notified of the change in schools and the decision to except a change is primarily in the hands of the foreign student advisor. In the case of an M-1 student, an application must be mailed to INS. You are not allowed to begin at the new school until 60 days after the submission of the application unless the application is approved prior to that time. If you cannot file prior to 60 days before classes begin in the new program, you must explain why you were unable to do so. Again, as a practical matter, an application which is filed prior to the transfer of schools would likely be approved by the INS, barring other negative factors.

EMPLOYMENT

Prior to the completion of your studies, as an M-1 student you are not allowed to accept employment in the United States. M-1 students are only eligible for post-completion practical training. You should submit a request for post-completion practical training, during the period which starts 60 days before the end of studies and ends no later than 30 days after completion of studies. You must apply to the INS for an employment authorization document (EAD) on Form I-765, with the correct fee, along with Form I-20 ID endorsed by the foreign student advisor. The INS will grant you practical training according to the following formula: one month of practical training for four months of M-1 study. The total period of post-completion practical training may not exceed six months. Permission to accept post-completion practical training will not be granted if the training applied for cannot be completed within the maximum period of time for which you are eligible.

CHANGING FROM M-1 STATUS

As an M-1 student you have limitations on your ability to change nonimmigrant status. You will not be able to change from M-1 to F-1 status unless you were issued an M-1 visa by mistake. An M-1 student who would like to study in the United States in F-1 status will have to leave the United States and reenter as an F-1 student and obtain an F-1 visa.

The rules for M-1 students changing to H-1 status are also different than those which apply to F-1's. An applicant for a change of status from M-1 student to H-1 worker cannot use educational training undertaken in M-1 status to meet the requirements for H-1 status. You can only change from M-1 to H-1 status if you have completed all the training necessary for the H-1 employment prior to enrolling in the M-1 training program.

The story of Eddie:

Eddie, from England, has the equivalent of a Masters degree in international finance. He has a job making a lot of money in a large bank in London but is totally bored with his job. What he would really like to do is study motorcycle repair so that he would link his favorite past time with a profession. He hopes some day to own a chain of motorcycle sales and repair shops in the United Kingdom. He learns of an excellent program in Miami, Florida in a vocational school and obtains an M-1 visa for the purpose of studying motorcycle repair. At the end of the four month program, Eddie obtains permission to engage in practical training and works for one month in a local motorcycle repair shop.

Since he has no immediate prospects of employment back in England, he decides he would like to try and stay in the United States for a while. He knows he can make a lot of money as an international investment banker and he knows that if he works hard and does well, in about three years time he will have enough money to go home to England and open his motorcycle shop. Eddie may begin working in the United States as an investment banker as soon as he obtains the change of status from M-1 to H-1B (see Chapter Eight). His application will be successful because he is not relying on any education he obtained in M-1 status to qualify for the H-1B status. He will only be using his education from England and once he establishes that he has the equivalent of a Bachelor degree or higher and that his job requires such a degree, he is able to obtain H-1B status and begin working. He cannot work in the United States as a motorcycle repair person because the H-1 status is specific to the employment with the bank in Florida as an investment banker.

Eddie does, however, join a motorcycle club, and part of the club's activities is a program teaching inner-city youth how to ride and repair motorcycles. Since he receives no compensation whatsoever for his activities with the motorcycle club, Eddie's work is not considered employment and he is not in violation of status.

CHAPTER SEVEN

J-1 Exchange Visitors

J-1 exchange visitor status is available to students, scholars, and researchers (as well as some business people, high school exchange students, college graduates, international camp counselors and others), through participation in a program administered through the United States Information Agency (USIA). Not every college or university has a J-1 program. While some programs are designed for Bachelors degree students, most are designed for graduate students, researchers and medical school students.

J-1 students commonly receive financial support from the U.S. government, their own government, or from the college or university they attend in the U.S. Under regulations which went into effect March 29, 1993, all new J-1 students must be substantially supported by other than personal funds. Some, but not all, J-1 exchange visitors are subject to a "two year home residence requirement" and cannot change their status to that of a temporary worker or U.S. permanent resident until they have satisfied the requirement or obtained a waiver of the requirement.

To qualify for J-1 status, you must be accepted into a J-1 program. The program sponsor, confirming acceptance, then issues Form IAP-66, Certificate of Eligibility for Exchange Visitor (J-1) status. The IAP-66 is presented to a consular officer abroad to obtain the J-1 visa. As a prospective J-1 student outside the U.S., you can sometimes obtain a B-2 visitor's visa where there is a delay in issuance of the IAP-66. In order to do so, you must satisfy the consul, usually with a letter from the program sponsor, that you have been accepted by a J-1 program. Prospective J-1 students, like F-1 students, are required to have a residence abroad that they do not intend to abandon.

OBTAINING J-1 STATUS THROUGH CONSULAR PROCESSING OR CHANGING STATUS

The procedures for obtaining J-1 status are essentially the same as for F-1 students, with the IAP-66 rather than the I-20 being the primary document establishing eligibility for the status. So, if you are a J-1 applicant, you should review chapters 1 through 4. Since most J-1 programs involve employment or financial assistance, it is often easier for the J-1 visa applicant to establish the necessary economic means to study and live in the United States.

MAINTENANCE OF STATUS

J-1 college and university students may apply to enroll in degree or non-degree programs. J-1 students are generally permitted to remain in the United States until their educational objectives have been completed. Additionally, J-1 college or university students may remain up to a maximum of 18 months after completion of studies (thirty-six months for post doctoral students) for practical training or what is now called "academic training". The sponsor may issue Form IAP-66 for varying periods of time, and extensions of stay may be required from your program sponsor along the way. Graduate medical students may stay for the length of their program or a maximum of seven years. Graduate nurses may stay for two years. Extensions of stay beyond these limits are available only in unusual circumstances.

Formerly, J-1 students were initially admitted to the United States for a specific period of time. New J-1 students are being admitted for "Duration of Status" or "D/S" similar to F-1 students. If you were admitted for a specific period of time and you are eligible for an extension, you must apply prior to the expiration of your stay. Your program sponsor will issue a new Form IAP-66. The new IAP-66 must be submitted to the INS with your and your dependents' original Form I-94, Form I-539, and a fee of $70.00 plus $10.00 for each of your dependents. If you are admitted for Duration of Status or D/S, there is no need to file an extension of stay request with the INS. Your program sponsor need only notify the USIA that the extension is granted.

PROGRAM TRANSFERS

J-1 students may transfer between programs provided that the two programs have similar objectives. Transfer requires the permission and signatures of both the current and prospective program sponsors.

SPOUSE AND DEPENDENTS OF J-I STUDENTS

As a J-1 exchange visitor, your spouse and unmarried minor children may accompany you to the U.S. and may remain with you so long as you are in lawful status. Unlike the F-2 dependent of the F-1 student, J-2 dependent spouses may apply to the INS for authorization to work. To receive employment authorization, they must show that they are working to meet their own or their children's financial needs and not to support the J-1 student or scholar. J-2 employment authorization may also be granted for the purpose of paying for entertainment or cultural activities of the family. The application for employment authorization should include an affidavit explaining financial and/or entertainment expenditure needs, personal income, and the need to work. This affidavit must accompany form I-765, Application for Employment Authorization. The application and supporting documents must be filed with the INS District Office having jurisdiction over your spouse's place of residence, with the filing fee of $60.00. Once the employment authorization is approved, your spouse will receive an employment authorization document (EAD), which is a photo-identification card.

J-1 EMPLOYMENT

For J-1 scholars, employment in J-1 status is often part of the program itself. As a J-1 student, you can work if you have the permission of your program sponsor. For pre-graduation employment, your program sponsor must find that the work will not interfere with your full time studies and (a) that your need to work arose after you came to the U.S. or (b) that your work is part of a fellowship, scholarship, or assistantship. J-1 students may not work for more than twenty hours per week while school is in session. Full time employment is only allowed during vacations. A program officer has great discretion in granting employment authorization, and policies in this regard vary from school to school. Once authorization is given by the program officer, permission from the INS is not required. For on campus employment, you must be maintaining a full course of studies.

THE TWO YEAR HOME PHYSICAL PRESENCE REQUIREMENT

You should carefully consider whether or not to participate in a J-1 exchange visitor program, because it may result in your becoming subject to the two year home resident requirement. If you become subject to this requirement, and you wish to either change status to that of an H-1A nurse, H-1B temporary professional worker, H-2 temporary worker, H-3 trainee, or an L-1 intracompany transferee, or wish to become a permanent resident of the United States, you will have to comply with this requirement or obtain a waiver prior to obtaining your new status. Compliance means returning to your home country for two years. Waivers, as described in more detail below, are often difficult to obtain.

WHO IS SUBJECT TO THE TWO YEAR FOREIGN RESIDENCE REQUIREMENT?

Not every J-1 exchange visitor is subject to the two-year requirement. An individual is subject to the two-year foreign residence requirement only if one of three situations apply:

(1) The exchange visitor's participation in the program was funded in whole or part, directly or indirectly, by a U.S. government agency or an agency of the government of an individual's home country.

A person who receives even a small amount of funds from an agency of their home government or the U.S. government is subject to the two-year foreign residence requirement.

(2) The skills developed as an exchange visitor are on the skills list of the exchange visitor's country.

Periodically, the Department of State inquires of governments throughout the world to determine whether or not there is a shortage of a particular skill or knowledge in their country. If your government indicates that certain skills are in short supply, that skill will be placed on what is known as the "skills list", and will be listed in the Foreign Affairs Manual (also called the "FAM") of the Department of State. This is significant because, if your skill was placed on the list after you entered the United States as a J-1 exchange visitor, you may be exempt from the two-year foreign residence requirement.

(3) The exchange visitor is a foreign medical graduate.

Foreign medical graduates or "FMGs" are people who come to the United States for graduate medical training. All J-1 foreign medical graduates are subject to the two year home residence requirement, except exchange visitors who come to this country to teach or do research. However, a teacher or researcher may be subject to the requirement if they are on the skills list, or if their J-1 program was funded by a U.S. government agency or the government of that person's country.

WAIVERS OF THE TWO-YEAR FOREIGN RESIDENCE REQUIREMENT

Once it is determined that a person is subject to the two-year foreign residence requirement, it does not necessarily mean that you will have to return home for two years prior to obtaining H-1A, H-1B, H-2, H-3, L-1, or permanent resident status. Under certain circumstances, you may be eligible for a waiver of the requirement. There are four types of waivers: no objection waiver; exceptional hardship waiver; persecution waiver; interested government agency waiver.

No objection waiver

You may be eligible for a waiver of the J-1 two-year foreign residence requirement if your country has "no objection". You should bear in mind that these waivers are generally not granted where the funding is from a U.S. government agency, but usually will be granted where the basis for requiring the waiver is the skills list and/or funding from an agency of your government. Where the funding is for a travel grant of less than $2,000, a no objection waiver may be granted even though your J-1 program was from a U.S. government source.

NOTE: The "no objection letter" waiver is not available to J-1 visa holders whose J-1 program was for the purpose of graduate medical education or training. The no objection waiver may be available to physicians who obtain a J-1 for the purpose of observation, consulting, teaching, or research.

The way to get a "no objection" waiver is to have the letter sent directly from the Embassy of your country to the USIA. It cannot be sent to the attorney or the alien and then forwarded to the USIA, but must be sent directly from the foreign government. The USIA will recommend for or against the waiver, and that recommendation will be forwarded to the INS District Office, where you live. While the INS will make an independent decision about the waiver, normally the recommendation of the USIA is followed.

Exceptional hardship waiver

If you are subject to the two-year foreign residence requirement, and you have a spouse or child who is a permanent resident or citizen of the United States, you can consider applying for a waiver of the two-year foreign residence requirement on the grounds of exceptional hardship. The application waiver is made directly to the INS, and you must establish that the U.S. citizen or permanent resident spouse or child will suffer great hardship if you are forced to live abroad for two years.

Economic hardship alone is generally not sufficient. However, where it can be established that separation will result in severe economic hardship or psychological or physical damage to the U.S. citizen spouse or child, or that such hardship will result if your spouse or child is required to accompany you abroad for two years, the waiver may be granted.

The most common ground for a hardship waiver is where the U.S. citizen or permanent resident spouse or child will suffer hardship as a result of a serious physical or mental disease or disability. Where you can establish an inability to obtain adequate medical treatment for your spouse or child in your home country, the waiver will usually be granted. Of course, the severity of the illness and the lack of adequate treatment in your home country must be well documented.

In support of the waiver application, you should include affidavits, marriage and/or birth certificates, letters from employers, psychologists, doctors, and other professionals as well as any other documentation to establish the validity of the claimed hardship.

The hardship waiver is submitted to the INS District Office where you live. The INS recommendation is then forwarded to the USIA for its decision on the waiver. The USIA usually follows the INS recommendation. However, a favorable INS recommendation where a J-1 medical doctor is applying for the waiver may be ignored by the USIA.

Persecution Waiver

If you can establish that you have a fear of persecution if you were to return home, you may be eligible for a waiver of the two-year foreign residence requirement. This waiver application is similar to an application for asylum. An exchange visitor considering a persecution waiver should also consider filing an application for asylum.

The persecution waiver application based on a fear of persecution is made to the USIA and its recommendation is forwarded to the INS. Again, as in the case of a "no objection" waiver, the INS will generally follow the recommendation of the USIA.

Interested government agency waiver

You may also obtain a waiver of the two-year foreign residence requirement where an interested government agency applies on your behalf. Obtaining a recommendation in support of the waiver application by the interested government agency involves establishing that your return home for two years will substantially affect research or other important work in which you are engaged in the United States. An interested government agency waiver is extremely difficult to obtain and is generally granted to aliens with outstanding and unique qualifications. Your employment must satisfy the government agency that your skills and/or knowledge are irreplaceable and that important research would suffer were you forced to return home.

HOW TO KNOW IF YOU ARE SUBJECT TO THE FOREIGN RESIDENCE REQUIREMENT

Often a person is not sure if he or she will be subject to the residence requirement. The visa page in the passport may or may not have an endorsement regarding the requirement. The Form IAP-66 (the pink form) may be improperly marked or not clearly marked.

To find out whether or not you are subject to the two year foreign residence requirement, consult with an attorney familiar with J-1 waivers. You may also send a copy of your IAP-66 Forms to the USIA and request an advisory opinion on the question. The USIA is not always correct in their determinations, but a letter from the USIA indicating that an individual is not subject to the foreign residence requirement is usually sufficient to establish this fact to the satisfaction of the INS.

The address of the USIA is: Waiver Review Office, USIA, 400 6th Street, S.W., Room 3030, Washington, D.C. 20547.

CHAPTER EIGHT

Temporary Professional Employment for College Graduates

After graduation, many foreign students wish to work temporarily in the United States. They are often interested in gaining experience which will be useful to them when they return to their countries of origin or see employment as a first step toward becoming a permanent resident. After post-completion practical training for F-1 students (see Chapter Five) or J-1 students (see Chapter Seven), a common avenue for temporary professional employment in the United States is H-1B status. For Canadians, additional possibilities exist because of the U.S.-Canada Free Trade Agreement.

WHAT IS H-1B STATUS?

H-1B status is a temporary status for aliens who wish to come to or remain in the United States to work in a professional position. This generally means individuals have to be offered a job where at least a Bachelors degree is a customary hiring requirement for the position. As a foreign worker, you must also demonstrate that you have obtained a

Bachelors degree or higher (or the equivalent in education or experience) in the particular field. The law refers to positions for H-1B status positions as "specialty occupations".

The Job Offered Must Be For A Position Where A Bachelors Degree Or Higher In A Particular Subject Is A Normal Minimum Job Requirement.

It is obvious that some positions almost always require a degree. Examples would be a college or university professor, an engineer, or an architect. Some positions are not so obvious. The position of manager of a small shoe store would not normally require a specific Bachelors degree and would not normally support an application for H-1B status. The position of accountant would usually require a degree in accounting and so would support an application for H-1B status.

Take the example of a small import-export company that might employ a multi-lingual secretary, a local sales representative, a buyer, and a manager. The secretary would probably not be considered a professional. The local sales representative and buyer might be considered professionals, but only if the buying and selling requires expertise normally acquired through a college education, such as the sale of engineering products or chemicals.

The manager may or may not be a professional. If the manager must understand international finance or law and the volume of business is such that a substantial amount of the manager's time is spent utilizing this knowledge, or like the jobs of buyer and seller, the manager's duties require special knowledge normally acquired through a college education, the position may be considered professional. If less than a Bachelors degree is generally required, the position will be considered non-professional.

The question of whether a position is considered professional depends on the job's duties and the skills required to perform those duties. If the job description clarifies the professional nature of the position and the employer can establish that he or she normally hires college graduates with specific degrees, or that similar businesses normally hire college graduates for similar positions, H-1B status will be available to the prospective employee.

The continuing story of Mary:

Mary's practical training is about to expire. She had no guarantee that her job teaching history at the community college would continue. So, she began looking for a job that would qualify her for H-1B status based on her new degree in political science. She looked for teaching jobs in a variety of subjects, including social science in a high school, history, and political science in colleges, and general education in a private elementary school. She also looked for a job as a researcher in the area of government or political science but was unsuccessful in all of these efforts. Finally, she obtained a job as an Editor for a publication which wrote and distributed comic books about civics for use in elementary schools.

While Mary had no experience in this area, her Bachelors degree in political science and the fact that she took several courses in United States government qualified her for the position. Her employer established that she was doing more than just correcting grammar and spelling since she was editing the text for factual accuracy. Her job also required research on the history and practice of U.S. government. So, even though her degree was in political science, she was deemed qualified for the position of Political Science and History Editor by the Immigration and Naturalization Service (INS), and the job was found to require the degree she had attained.

The Alien Must Possess The Minimum Qualifications

An applicant for H-1B status based on a professional position must possess the equivalent of a U.S. Bachelors degree or higher, or must have sufficient experience and education combined to be considered the equivalent of a college degree or higher.

The degree, however, must be in an area of professional expertise required by the position offered. Someone with a degree in chemistry would qualify for H-1B status as a chemist but not as a social worker. The area of business or business administration is so broad that a degree in business may or may not qualify the alien for a position offered in the absence of a concentration in a particular area, such as accounting or finance.

The continuing story of James:

James managed to get his degree in business management but just barely. In his last year, he spent most of his time going to parties and participating in the student government at the college and as a result his grades suffered. He did graduate, but he was near the bottom of his class. He was eligible for and obtained post-completion practical training and got a job working in a hotel but as a result of the recession, he was laid off.

He had great difficulty in finding another job and finally through a friend of his uncle's back home, he was able to find a position as an entry level junior hotel management executive. The

job required a college degree in business administration or Hotel Management but did not require experience. Even though the employer had not been advertising, he routinely got 30 to 40 letters per week from applicants looking for a position. Nevertheless, because the employer was a friend of James' uncle, he offered James the position and petitioned for him for H-1B status. James applied to change from F-1 to H-1B status and was successful. Even though there may be hundreds of workers qualified for the position, James is also qualified for the position by virtue of his having a Bachelors degree in business. Since H-1B status does not require the showing of the unavailability of lawful U.S. workers, James should be able to obtain H-1B status if the other requirements for that status are met. His change of status is approved for a period of three years and he may later extend that for an additional three years for a total of six years.

There Must Be An Offer Of Employment

No H-1B petition is approved without a United States employer or agent offering employment. The employer may be an individual, partnership, or corporation. Sometimes a corporation, solely or majority owned by one individual, will petition for that same individual claiming he or she is also an employee of the corporation. This may be acceptable if the business is properly incorporated, the job offer is bona fide, and all other requirements for an H-1B petition are met. However, petitions by new corporations with limited capitalization are carefully scrutinized by the INS to insure that the corporation was not created solely to provide employment for its owner.

The Labor Condition Application (LCA) Requirement for H-1B Workers

The 1990 Immigration Act amended the requirements and procedures for H-1B classification. These changes became effective October 1, 1991.

The law now requires prospective H-1B employers to file a labor condition application or "LCA" with the Department of Labor before an H-1B petition can be filed with the INS. The employer must attest to certain conditions in this application: that the employer will pay the higher of the prevailing or actual wage for the position, or that the employer will offer prevailing working conditions to the prospective H-1B alien and to all other H-1B workers in the same job category at the employer's facility; and that the employer has posted a notice of filing the H-1B attestation in two conspicuous locations at the place of employment or notify the collective bargaining agent, as applicable. The employer must also keep records proving that the statements made in the LCA are true.

THE PROCEDURE FOR OBTAINING H-1 STATUS

In order for you, as a prospective employee to qualify for H-1B status, your employer must have an H-1B petition approved on your behalf. The first step in the process is obtaining the prevailing wage for the job and determining the actual wage your employer normally pays for the position. Prevailing wage may be obtained through a request to the state department of labor (referred to as a "SESA" for state employment security agency) or by using an independent authoritative wage survey or union contract. Once your employer obtains the prevailing wage, the next step is to prepare the LCA. Your employer must post notice regarding the filing of the H-1B petition in at least two locations at his or her place of business for ten days. Many employers use an LCA form itself for the posting. An employer is required to maintain documentation regarding the wages paid to H-1B workers and other workers doing the same job and must demonstrate that you are to be paid the higher of the actual or prevailing wage.

After the posting of the notice, two copies of the LCA are filed with the U.S. Department of Labor. After the LCA is certified as received, a process that can take up to two weeks, the H-1B petition may then be filed with the INS with supporting documents that would include a copy of the original certified LCA, proof of your educational background and/or experience, and the job description.

If you are in the United States, you can apply for a change of status. If you are abroad, a notice of approval of the petition may be sent to a U.S. consulate.

Other Considerations Regarding H-1B Status

An H-1B petition can be granted initially by the INS for up to three years and can be extended for a total of three additional years. In most parts of the country, petition approval will take about four weeks. In an emergency, in some parts of the United States, an H-1B petition may be approved more quickly, but to obtain an expeditious decision your employer will need to establish a substantial business necessity, with a clear explanation as to the unforeseen circumstances that led to the need for a speedy decision.

The employer does not have to establish that there are no U.S. workers to fill the position offered. Unlike some other visas for employment purpose in the United States, an employer can petition for H-1B status for an employee even if a qualified U.S. citizen or permanent resident is available for the position.

CONVINCING AN EMPLOYER TO SPONSOR AN INDIVIDUAL FOR H-1B STATUS

Some employers are reluctant to hire graduating foreign students, despite the fact that you may come to the employer already eligible to work with post-completion practical training. The reason is often a fear that it will be difficult for the employer to petition for you to continue employment beyond your one year's practical training period. It is worth remembering that while help of an attorney is often required, most H-1B petitions are approved with little inconvenience to the employer.

Most importantly, you must emphasize to your employer that there is no requirement that says you must be outstanding, unique, or that there is a shortage of lawful U.S. workers available to fill the position.

"TC" STATUS FOR CANADIAN PROFESSIONALS

A Canadian entering the United States to perform certain professional services does not need to petition for H-1B status if he or she is deemed eligible to enter as a "TC" under the Free Trade Agreement between the United States and Canada. Most professions approved for TC status require a college degree or Canadian provincial license. In some cases, experience is accepted in lieu of education. A list of professions indicated in the TC category can be obtained from a U.S. immigration attorney or U.S. consulate in Canada. A list for 1992 is found in the appendix.

One advantage of entering in TC status as opposed to H-1B status is that the employer need not file a petition with INS on behalf of the TC. If you qualify, you need only present yourself at certain United States ports of entry with a letter from a U.S. employer confirming the details of the position offered and proof of your qualifications. Another advantage is that if you can demonstrate a permanent home in Canada to which you intend to return, you can obtain an unlimited number of annual extensions of stay, unlike the six year limit for H-1B status.

CHAPTER NINE

Other Nonimmigrant Visas

People may come to the United States in a number of nonimmigrant visa categories for a variety of purposes. Visitors for business or pleasure may come to the United States in B-1 or B-2 status. In particular, individuals considering study in the United States who have not identified a college they would like to attend (or have yet to be accepted into a college) may use a B-2 visa to come to the United States and then change status to F-1, M-1, or J-1. Foreign students who would like to work in the United States may wish to change their status either prior to or upon graduation. In addition to H-1B status discussed in the previous Chapter, H-2, H-3, E-1, E-2, O, P, and R status may be available to an individual seeking to work in the United States.

A list of nonimmigrant visas can be found in the appendix.

B-1 VISITOR FOR BUSINESS, B-2 VISITOR FOR PLEASURE

B-1 visas are available for individuals coming to the United States for business purposes. Examples include setting up a new enterprise, taking orders or providing other services for a foreign company, or attending a professional conference.

B-2 visas are available for individuals coming to the United States on vacation, to attend a family event such as a wedding or funeral, and for other non-commercial activities. It is also available to prospective students coming to the United States to investigate colleges or universities for possible future attendance.

B-1 and B-2 visas are not required for citizens of Andorra, Austria, Belgium, Canada, Denmark, Finland, France, Germany, Iceland, Italy, Japan, Liechtenstein, Luxembourg, Monaco, the Netherlands, New Zealand, Norway, San Marino, Spain, Sweden, Switzerland, and the United Kingdom. If you come from one of these countries you can enter the United States without a B-1/B-2 visa and remain here for a period of no longer than 90 days under the "visa waiver program". If you enter the United States under this program, you cannot change to another nonimmigrant status while in the United States.

In order to obtain a B-1 or B-2 visa, you need to establish that you only intend to visit the United States temporarily and that you have a residence abroad that you have no intention of abandoning (see "Proving Nonimmigrant Intent" in Chapter Two for more information).

H-2B TEMPORARY WORKER

This status is for individuals who will provide temporary services to an employer. Short term and start-up projects often have positions that can be considered temporary. H-2 status requires proof of the unavailability of lawful U.S. workers. The status may be granted for a period up to one year at a time with a three year time limit. It is often very difficult to obtain H-2 status and even more difficult to obtain an extension of stay beyond one year.

The story of Francesco:

Francesco, from Florence, Italy is a skilled artisan. He has ten years experience making marble table tops with complicated engravings. An American company would like him to come to the United States for one year to assist in developing their new line of Italian marble table tops. The project will involve making table tops, as well as training U.S. workers. It is anticipated that within that year, the Italian style marble table production unit of the U.S. company will be on its feet and will no longer need Francesco's services. Francesco's U.S. employer, with the help of a lawyer, advertises and establishes that there are no individuals in the Cincinnati area where the company is located who have the necessary experience and willingness to perform the job they would like to offer Francesco. Once it is established that there are no available U.S. workers and that Francesco will be paid the normal wage for the job offered, a temporary labor certification application is approved valid for one year and an H-2B petition is filed with the Immigration and Naturalization Service (INS) and that too is approved. The approved petition is forwarded to the U.S. consul in Florence where Francesco obtains an H-2B visa valid for one year.

H-3 TRAINEE

H-3 status is available for an alien in a training program not available in the alien's home country. There is a two year time limitation on H-3 status, and the H-3 worker need not have a college degree. There are strict requirements as to proof of the nature of the training program, and the trainer must establish that the trainee will not be displacing a U.S. worker. The trainer must also establish that any productive work performed by the trainee is secondary to the training process.

The story of Vanessa:

Vanessa, from Venezuela, wants to participate in a two year training program for account executives in a major international stock brokerage company based in the United States. Vanessa can obtain an H-3 visa to participate in the program which will pay her $30,000 a year. To obtain the H-3 status, the employer/trainer will have to establish that there is an organized training program with a detailed explanation as to in class instruction and reading materials required, the subjects that will be considered, and the process for evaluation. It will not be enough to say that Vanessa will learn on the job during those two years. The employer will also have to establish that the training Vanessa receives is unavailable in Venezuela. Since she is learning U.S. stock and commodities training, this should be no problem. In fact, the purpose of the program is to train people for employment in the foreign offices of the U.S. company. The company must also establish the primary purpose of Vanessa's employment is training, not creating immediate profits for the company.

E-1 TREATY TRADER / E-2 TREATY INVESTOR

E visa status is based on treaties between the United States and an alien's country of nationality. Not all foreign countries have entered into agreements with the United States qualifying their nationals for E-1 or E-2 status. Some countries have E-1 or E-2 eligibility, but not both.

E-1 Treaty Trader status is based on a treaty of trade and commerce between the United States and another country. To qualify for E-1 status, the U.S. organization must be at least 50% owned by nationals of the treaty country, the organization must be principally (at least 51% of the volume of business) engaged in trade between the United States and the treaty country, the trade must be substantial, and the alien must be entering the United States to serve in a capacity that is managerial or involves essential skills.

E-2 Investor status is based on an investment by one or more foreign nationals. As in the case of the E-1, the U.S. organization must be at least 50% owned by nationals of the treaty country. The investment cannot be passive (e.g. bank accounts, undeveloped land) and must be "substantial". An investment that only supports the investor and his or her family is considered marginal and will not qualify for E-2 status. E-2 status is available to the investor to direct and develop the enterprise and to employees of the investor who will function in a managerial capacity or who have special skills necessary to the development of the investment.

E-1 Treaty Trader status is available to nationals of Argentina, Australia, Austria, Belgium, Bolivia, Brunei, Canada, China, Colombia, Costa Rica, Denmark, Estonia, Ethiopia, Finland, France, Germany, Greece, Honduras, Iran, Ireland, Israel, Italy, Japan, Latvia, Liberia, Luxembourg, the Netherlands, Norway, Oman, Pakistan, Paraguay, the Philippines, Republic of Korea, Spain, Suriname, Sweden, Switzerland, Thailand, Togo, Turkey, the United Kingdom, and Yugoslavia.

E-2 Treaty Investor status is available to nationals of Argentina, Australia, Austria, Bangladesh, Belgium, Cameroon, Canada, Colombia, Costa Rica, Ethiopia, France, Germany, Grenada, Honduras, Iran, Italy, Japan, Liberia, Luxembourg, Morocco, the Netherlands, Norway, Oman, Pakistan, Paraguay, the Philippines, Republic of Korea, Senegal, Spain, Suriname, Sweden, Switzerland, Thailand, Togo, Turkey, the United Kingdom, Yugoslavia, and Zaire.

O STATUS FOR INDIVIDUALS OF EXTRAORDINARY ABILITY

The O visa category includes individuals of extraordinary ability in the sciences, arts, education, business, or athletics, as demonstrated by sustained national or international acclaim, or with regard to motion picture and television production, a demonstrated record of extraordinary achievements recognized in the field through documentation.

These visas are also available to individuals who themselves are not extraordinary but who accompany an O individual and assist in an artistic or athletic performance for a special event or events. The individual must be an integral part of the performance and have critical skills and experience with the principal performer or athlete, not of a general nature, which cannot be performed by others.

THE P VISA CATEGORY FOR ATHLETES AND ENTERTAINERS

The P visa category allows an alien to enter the United States to perform as an athlete at an internationally recognized level of performance or as part of an entertainment group that has been recognized internationally as outstanding in the field. Additionally, there are provisions for performances in exchange programs and unique cultural programs. Admission periods in P status can be for an initial period of up to five years, with an extension for up to five years.

R STATUS FOR RELIGIOUS WORKERS

The R visa category is available to aliens (and their accompanying immediate family) entering the United States to carry on activities as religious workers. The status is available for a period not in excess of five years for a minister, a professional religious worker, or a person in a religious vocation or occupation, such as an liturgical worker, cantor, or missionary. To qualify for an R visa, an individual must have been a member of the religious denomination making the application for at least the two years immediately preceding the application for admission. In addition, the R nonimmigrant must show that he or she is qualified in the religious occupation or vocation. The initial period of time granted to an R worker will be for a maximum of three years. An additional two years may be requested subsequently.

CHAPTER TEN

Permanent Residence

During their stay in the United States, many foreign students consider the possibility of remaining permanently. In this Chapter, we very briefly explore the possibilities available to an individual seeking permanent residence in the United States.

WHAT IS A PERMANENT RESIDENT?

A permanent resident ("green card" holder) may reside indefinitely in the United States, work in most jobs (the exception being some government jobs), petition for certain relatives to become permanent residents, and, if desired, eventually become a citizen of the United States.

PERMANENT RESIDENCE BASED ON EMPLOYMENT

Many people are able to become permanent residents of the United States because they possess skills, education, or outstanding talent needed in the United States. Overall, a total of 140,000 visas are available each year to the five groupings of immigrants described below. If you seek residence based on an offer of employment, you will generally be able to do so more quickly than in the past for all categories -- with the exception of the "lesser skilled" worker subcategory. These lesser skilled workers are people whose jobs require less than two years of training or experience. Visas are limited to 10,000 annually for lesser skilled workers, and processing for permanent residence could well take six years or more.

Note that in some visa categories a sponsoring employer must establish the unavailability of lawful U.S. workers willing, ready, and able to accept the job offered. This process is known as labor certification and is described in greater detail below.

First Employment-Based Preference: Priority Workers

No labor certification is required for first preference workers, which are broken down into three types:

- **Aliens With Extraordinary Ability** in the sciences, arts, education, business, or athletics, as demonstrated by sustained national or international acclaim with recognized achievements supported by extensive documentation. You must intend to continue working in the area of extraordinary ability, and your entry must prospectively substantially benefit the United States.

- **Outstanding Professors and Researchers** with international recognition as outstanding in a specific academic area and at least three years experience in teaching or research in the academic area.

- **Multinational Executives and Managers** who have been employed, for at least one year during the three years preceding the filing of a petition, by a company abroad (or its subsidiary or affiliate), and seek to enter the United States to continue to render services to the same employer or a subsidiary or affiliate thereof in a managerial or executive capacity.

Second Employment-Based Preference: Aliens who are (a) Members of Professions Holding Advanced Degrees or (b) of Exceptional Ability

The second preference applies to members of the professions holding advanced degrees (or in some circumstances their equivalent). It also includes aliens who because of their exceptional ability in the sciences, arts, or business will substantially benefit the national economy, cultural, educational interests, or welfare of the United States.

In this category, an employer must establish the unavailability of U.S. workers. In limited instances, when the national interest is at stake, the job offer requirement can be waived.

Third Employment-Based Preference: Skilled Workers, Professionals, and "Other" Workers

The third preference covers a wide range of workers:

- **Skilled workers** are aliens capable of performing labor requiring at least two years education, training, or experience.

- **Professionals** are qualified individuals who hold a U.S. Bachelors degree or the academic equivalent and who are members of the professions.

- **"Other" Workers** (including lesser skilled workers) are aliens performing unskilled labor requiring less than two years training or experience. Not more than 10,000 visas annually may be used by these "other workers".

In this category, an employer must establish the unavailability of U.S. workers by obtaining a labor certification.

Fourth Employment-Based Preference: "Special Immigrants"

Religious workers with two years experience such as ministers, religious professionals and some religious non-professionals may qualify as "special immigrants".

Other special immigrants include former U.S. government employees (under certain circumstances), Panama Canal employees, certain foster children who are juvenile dependents of the Court, and dependents of diplomats.

Fifth Employment-Based Preference: Investors

The fifth preference, "employment creation", refers to alien investors who engage in a new commercial enterprise, established by the alien, in which the alien has invested or is in the process of investing capital. The enterprise must create full-time employment for at least ten U.S. citizens or permanent residents.

Of the 10,000 visa numbers available in this category, at least 3,000 are set aside for aliens who establish enterprises in a "targeted" employment area, defined as a rural area or area which has experienced high unemployment.

The stated amount of capital required is set at $1 million. However, for targeted areas, the Attorney General has specified a required amount of capital of only $500,000. For an investment made in a metropolitan area that is not targeted, but has an unemployment rate significantly below the national average, the Attorney General may increase the amount above $1 million.

If you receive immigration benefits under this section, you will receive conditional residence and must apply to the Immigration and Naturalization Service (INS) to have the condition removed within the 90 day period preceding the two year anniversary of getting your green card.

THE LABOR CERTIFICATION REQUIREMENT IN EMPLOYMENT RELATED PERMANENT RESIDENT CASES

When an individual labor certification is required for an employment-based immigrant visa, an application is filed with the U.S. Department of Labor. The employer must show efforts to recruit qualified lawful U.S. workers to fill the position, normally by advertising the position. The employer must establish that there is no qualified U.S. worker available for the position.

Applications for college and university teachers are treated under special rules. Here, the employer need only establish that a competitive search was made within eighteen months prior to filing and the alien was best qualified for the position. There is no need to show the unavailability of minimally qualified U.S. workers.

Many employers believe that, in order to apply for a labor certification, the alien must be unique or outstanding. This is not the case. In fact, many professional, skilled, and semi-skilled positions can be used as a basis to obtain permanent residence.

As a general rule, if it is difficult for an employer to find a qualified U.S. worker to fill a particular position, there is a good chance of obtaining a labor certification for an alien to fill that position so long as the employer is paying the prevailing wage for the position.

The employer must make a bona fide (honest and genuine) offer of employment. If an employee fails to actually begin employment, quits after a short time, or is fired, the employer is not liable or responsible.

PERMANENT RESIDENCE BASED ON FAMILY RELATIONSHIPS

The following individuals are eligible to apply for permanent residence based on family relationships:

- **The spouse of a U.S. citizen or lawful permanent resident.** Note that aliens who obtain residence based on a marriage within two years of the date of the marriage are called "conditional residents". Conditional residence is valid for two years. An additional application to the INS is required to have the condition removed.

- **The children of U.S. citizens.** This category includes children of any age, single or married. A qualifying parent/child relationship may include certain adopted children, step-children, or children born out-of-wedlock.

- **The parent of a U.S. citizen** if the U.S. citizen child is 21 years of age or older. (See #2 above regarding parent/child relationship.)

- **The unmarried children, any age, of a lawful permanent resident.** (See #2 above re: parent/child relationship.) An unmarried child may be one who is divorced or widowed at the time the petition is filed.

- **The brother or sister of a U.S. citizen** if the U.S. citizen is over 21 years of age.

Note that, for both employment and family based eligibility for permanent residence, some categories have very long (two to ten years or longer) waiting lines, and permanent resident status in the United States cannot be obtained until long after the process is started.

LOTTERY OR DIVERSITY VISAS

Beginning October 1, 1991, 40,000 visas a year became available for individuals from countries where immigration to the United States has been less than average in the past 25 years. Beginning in 1995, 55,000 visas per year will be given to individuals from areas with low amounts of immigration during the previous five years.

People who were born within the following countries were entitled to apply for the lotteries: Albania, Algeria, Argentina, Austria, Belgium, Bermuda, Canada, Czechoslovakia, Denmark, Estonia, Finland, France, Germany, Gibraltar, Great Britain, Guadeloupe, Hungary, Iceland, Indonesia, Ireland, Italy, Japan, Latvia, Liechtenstein, Lithuania, Luxembourg, Monaco, the Netherlands, New Caledonia, Northern Ireland, Norway, Poland, San Marino, Sweden, Switzerland, and Tunisia.

To become a permanent resident based on the 1992-1994 lotteries, you must have a firm employment commitment in the United States for at least one year and be otherwise admissible. Forty percent of the visas awarded in each of the three years will go to applicants from Ireland and Northern Ireland.

The second diversity program will make available 55,000 "diversity visas" each year commencing in 1995 to applicants from areas with low levels of immigrant admissions from 1992-1995 and thereafter. There is a complicated formula for determining how the visas will be distributed to each country. The highest number of visas will be given to low admission states which are located in low admission parts of the world. Nationals of countries which had high numbers of admissions into the United States (over 50,000 lawful permanent residents) will not receive diversity immigrant visas under the diversity program. Applicants must have a high school diploma or two years of work experience in an occupation that requires at least two years of training or experience.

OTHER POSSIBILITIES FOR PERMANENT RESIDENCE

Registry

In addition to the categories described above, a person who entered the United States before January 1, 1972 and who has resided continuously in the United States since that entry may apply for registry.

Last resorts

Alternative forms of relief described below are difficult to obtain but may be considered as a last resort. These forms of relief may allow you to stay in the United States and get employment authorization.

Asylum

A person may be eligible for asylum who can establish a well-founded fear of persecution if compelled to return to his or her home country, if the persecution is based on political opinion, religion, race, national origin, or membership in a social group. A successful asylum applicant is eligible to apply for permanent residence after one year. Only a small percentage of asylum applications are granted by the INS. Applications for asylum can be renewed before, or made in, the first instance to an immigration judge if the applicant is in exclusion or deportation proceedings.

Suspension of Deportation

A person who has resided continuously in the United States for seven years may, under very special circumstances such as extreme hardship, be eligible for suspension of deportation. A person granted suspension of deportation can become a permanent resident. Suspension of deportation requires a showing of extreme hardship to an alien or their U.S. citizen or permanent resident spouse, parent, or child. Suspension of deportation is available only to those in deportation proceedings. A person denied suspension of deportation may be ordered deported.

Private Bills

This is an extreme and unusual remedy which is very rarely granted. A private bill is an act of Congress granting permanent residence to an individual where no other remedy is available to the alien, and extraordinary humanitarian factors exist.

CHAPTER ELEVEN

Special Rules for Special Nationalities

Occasionally, spurred by civil strife or disaster in a foreign country, the U.S. Congress, the President or the INS establish special programs to assist the victims of these events. In this chapter, we identify and explain some of these special programs.

NATIONALS OF THE PEOPLE'S REPUBLIC OF CHINA (PRC)

On April 11, 1990, then President George Bush issued an executive order which provided for employment authorization and extended stay for nationals of the People's Republic of China (PRC) who were present in the United States on or after June 5, 1989, up to and including April 11, 1990. The executive order was intended to assure nationals of the PRC in the United States that they would not be forced to return to China against their will before January 1, 1994. Protection was extended to all Chinese present in the United States as of those dates or if not present, those whose temporary stay was interrupted by a brief, casual and innocent departure.

The status provided under this special program is called deferred departure status for PRC nationals. Deferred departure status provides permission to remain in and work in the United States up to January 1, 1994. It does not give automatic permission to reenter the United States after travel abroad. Travel permission may be obtained from the INS separately. The permission to travel is called advance parole.

Under "deferred departure status," any PRC national who was in the United States in legal status on or after June 5, 1989, up to and including April 11, 1990, will be considered to have maintained lawful status. PRC nationals who leave the United States for immigrant visa processing do not require unexpired passports to be issued an immigrant visa, and they can enter the U.S. if they were granted advanced parole.

WAIVER OF THE TWO YEAR HOME RESIDENCE REQUIREMENT FOR J-1 EXCHANGE VISITORS

Many PRC nationals in the United States are subject to the two year home residence requirement for J-1 exchange visitors (see Chapter 7). President Bush's executive order provided an irrevocable waiver of the requirement for PRC nationals eligible for deferred departure status. To obtain a waiver, you must apply for a change in status to any nonimmigrant status for which you are eligible or must apply for adjustment of status to permanent residence on or before January 1, 1994. The waiver does not apply to a person who changed status from J-1 to another nonimmigrant status and thereafter either changed their status to J-1 or entered the U.S. in a new J-1 status.

THE CHINESE STUDENT PROTECTION ACT (CSPA)

Nationals of the PRC who were present in the United States at any time between June 5, 1989, and April 11, 1990 and who have resided continuously in the U.S. since that time can qualify for permanent residence under the Chinese Student Protection Act (CSPA). You don't have to be a student to qualify, nor do you have to have applied for the "deferred departure status" for Chinese nationals described above. But, you have to have been inspected at entry by an INS officer upon your last arrival in the U.S. If you were in the PRC for more than 90 days at any time between June 5, 1989, and April 11, 1990, you are not qualified for permanent residence under this program. Having been subject to the two year home residence requirement for J-1 Exchange Visitors will not disqualify you from permanent resident under the CSPA.

Applications under the CSPA were accepted beginning July 1, 1993. The final day to apply will be June 30, 1994. Applications, and the address of the INS Regional Service Center where the application must be filed, can be obtained at your local INS office. The filing fee is $120. Any applications to the INS should be sent certified mail/return receipt requested and a photocopy kept for your records.

In most cases, no interview will be required. If your application is approved, you will be notified by mail and you can then take your approval notice with your passport to your local INS district office to have it stamped with temporary evidence of permanent residence. This stamp will permit you to travel while you are waiting for your Alien Registration Card (green card). The green card should be sent to you two to six months after you receive your approval notice by registered mail.

If you need to travel outside of the U.S. while your CSPA application is pending, you must apply for advance parole at your local INS district office. You may have to show an urgent family, professional or business need to travel.

TEMPORARY PROTECTED STATUS (TPS)

The Immigration Act of 1990 created a temporary status for certain victims of civil strife or natural disaster. For designated countries, an individual in the United States may be granted the right to remain in the United States with employment authorization until the status is lifted. The 1990 law also established a special program for nationals of El Salvador. The status is known as temporary protected status or "TPS". TPS does not have any effect on valid nonimmigrant status. For example, if an F-1 student applies for TPS available to nationals of Lebanon for example, the mere fact of applying for TPS does not remove that individual from valid F-1 status. The F-1 status continues. When the TPS ends and you are out of status, you may be subject to deportation proceedings.

If you intend to apply for TPS status, you should consult with a foreign student advisor, attorney, or authorized representative. Countries whose nationals have been eligible (and in some cases may still be) for TPS includes El Salvador, Lebanon, Kuwait, Liberia, Somalia, and Bosnia-Hercegovina.

To qualify for TPS, an individual must: (a) have entered the United States before the qualifying dates; (b) registered for TPS during the open registration periods; (c) have not been convicted of a felony or two or more misdemeanors in the United States; and (d) be admissible as an immigrant.

Applications for TPS must be made at an INS office having jurisdiction over the place of residence of the applicant. An applicant for TPS must present to the INS:

a. Form I-765, Application for Employment Authorization;

b. Two fingerprint cards to be completed;

c.   Two passport size photographs;

d.   Form I-821, TPS Eligibility Questionnaire;

e.   Proof of citizenship of the TPS country, such as a passport or national identity document or a baptismal certificate;

f.   Proof of continuous residence in the United States on or before the designated date. For example, payroll stubs, rent receipts, and postdated envelopes that are addressed to you;

g.   Check or money order for the amount of the fee applicable in your case (a fee varies according to the country of which you are a national).

It is important to note that TPS does not lead to permanent residence. However, the grant of employment authorization is helpful. In order for you to find an employer who is willing to sponsor you for permanent residence, the grant of employment authorization is often a sufficient period of time to allow you to process a labor certification and employment-based immigrant visa petition.

PART
II

PART

II

CHAPTER TWELVE

Your Legal Rights and Responsibilities

Foreign students -- in fact, any individual who has entered the United States, even someone who came without any papers at all -- have many of the same rights and obligations as U.S. citizens. They can sue and be sued, they can be charged with a crime, be convicted and be sentenced to fines or imprisonment and, in a criminal case, have the right to a court appointed counsel if they cannot afford their own lawyer. Even if you are planning to spend a relatively short time in the United States, it is well worth your time becoming acquainted with U.S. laws and our legal system.

In general, nonimmigrants in the United States (such as foreign students and scholars) enjoy the same constitutional protections as U.S. citizens. They enjoy freedom of speech, freedom of assembly, protection from unreasonable searches and seizures, and the other protections included in the "Bill of Rights" of the U.S. Constitution. They can own property (land and buildings) if they wish to, and they are protected against discrimination on the grounds of race, religion, color, and national origin. There are federal, state, and often municipal rules protecting all persons from most forms of discrimination.

CIVIL LAWS, COURTS AND LAWYERS

If you have been wronged by another and can prove that you were damaged as a result, you may have the right to sue the wrongdoer in court for monetary damages. The person suing is called the plaintiff, and the person being sued is called the defendant. The fact that you are not a U.S. citizen will not affect your rights. If you are hit by a car and injured and it was not your fault, or if you were unfairly treated in a business deal, you may have the right to sue to recover damages. In many cases, there is a statute of limitations which will prevent you from suing another person if you wait too long to sue after the incident. If you are injured physically or financially and you are considering suing the person who injured you, it is best to consider doing so soon after the injury occurs.

Lawyers

With the exception of small claims court, described below, you will probably need a lawyer to represent you if you wish to sue an individual who has injured you. Lawyers generally charge for their services in one of three ways: a contingency fee, an hourly fee, and a flat fee. The fee agreement will often depend on the kind of case you have.

If you are hit by a car or fall down slippery stairs and would like to sue the party responsible for your injuries, your lawyer will most often take the case on a "contingency basis". This means that your lawyer will not charge you for his or her services (which are distinguished from expenses) unless money is recovered on your behalf. The lawyer's fee will be a percentage of the money recovered from the person or company that caused the injury.

Suppose someone sues you. If you have insurance covering that type of accident, your insurance company will have a lawyer represent you and you will not have to pay the legal fees. If you do not have insurance and you hire a lawyer, the lawyer may charge you on an hourly basis and ask for a specified amount (called a retainer) to start. Every time the lawyer does work for you, including talking to you on the phone, he or she will keep track of the time spent and charge you for it. Hourly fees are generally charged when a lawyer is not sure how much time will be spent on a case, and is not representing a party likely to recover damages.

When a case is routine and the lawyer can easily determine how much time to spend on the case, he or she may charge a flat fee or set fee. That is, a fee you and the lawyer agree to in advance. Many immigration cases, uncontested divorces and simple bankruptcy cases are charged on a flat fee basis.

If you cannot afford a lawyer and your case is not one which a lawyer would normally take on a contingency fee basis as described above, you should speak to a foreign student advisor about the availability of free or low cost legal services in your area. Some colleges have a legal service plan prepaid for out of student activities fees. Since individuals in the United States in nonimmigrant status are not eligible for federally funded legal services in civil cases, community and social service organizations around the country have developed to provide legal assistance in deportation defense, divorce, child custody, and housing. These programs are especially designed to meet the needs of the immigrant population.

Small Claims Court

One type of court action in which you ordinarily do not need a lawyer is small claims court. Small claims court is designed to provide speedy relief for a person where a relatively small amount of money is involved. Generally the maximum you are allowed to sue for in small claims court is between $500 and $2000. If you believe that someone owes you money of this amount or less, you should visit the small claims court, and the clerk will assist you in preparing the proper papers and notifying the party you are suing. The fee for filing a claim in small claims court is usually very low, and court hearings are often held at night.

CRIMINAL CASES

A foreign student has even more reason than a U.S. citizen to be concerned about the ramifications of criminal activity. A U.S. citizen who is convicted of a crime may face a fine or imprisonment. The foreign student will suffer these penalties and may be deported as well.

Some foreign students fear that if they are convicted — or even accused — of a violation of any law they will be deported immediately and automatically. That is not true. Not all arrests and convictions will result in serious immigration consequences for a foreign student, and every person has a right to a hearing before being deported from the United States. For some people convicted of a deportable offense, a waiver of deportation may be available.

A conviction for disorderly conduct, petty theft, disturbing the peace, drunkenness, or a similar minor offense will normally not seriously affect an individual's status in the United States. Conviction for any offense involving illegal drugs, on the other hand, normally will have grave immigration consequences. The same is true for crimes such as burglary, robbery, and rape. Obviously the best way to avoid the immigration consequences of criminal activity is not to engage in any.

If you are arrested or charged with a crime, you or your criminal attorney should consult with an immigration lawyer before pleading guilty to any charges.

Your Rights if Arrested or Accused of a Crime

A foreign student has the same rights as a U.S. citizen if accused of a crime: the right to be represented by a lawyer, and to be provided with a lawyer to represent you if you cannot afford to hire one; the right to remain silent or not to answer questions asked by a law enforcement officer regarding your possible involvement in criminal activity; and the right not to be searched unless the police officer has a warrant, except in emergency circumstances. If you are accused of having committed a crime, the best advice in most circumstances is to not answer any questions regarding charges until you have had the opportunity to talk to a lawyer.

Your Right to Freedom of Speech and Religion

Foreign students have the constitutional right to express their views freely, to join together with others in the expression of those views, and to participate fully in the propagation and publication of ideas, popular or unpopular, so long as those expressions are made in an orderly and peaceful manner. They have the same rights to free speech and are subject to the same limitations of freedom of action as are U.S. citizens.

INCOME TAX

Special provisions of the Internal Revenue Code apply to nonimmigrants in F, M, and J status. Certain income of F, M, or J visa holders may be exempt from tax payment.

In general, the Internal Revenue Service or "IRS" considers F, M, or J visa holders to be non-resident aliens for the purposes of tax payments. However, there are exceptions to this rule. For example, if you have been in the United States in either the F, M, or J categories for more than four of the last six years, you may be considered to be a resident alien for tax purposes. Resident aliens are taxed in the same manner as U.S. citizens.

A non-resident alien is usually subject to U.S. income tax only on income from sources within the United States. For students in the F, M, or J categories, certain income received from abroad or from foreign employers may be received from abroad or from foreign employers may be exempt from income tax in the United States. Income derived from sources within the United States is generally taxable.

Foreign students should be aware that the United States has income treaties or agreements with a number of foreign countries. Under these treaties, residents of the foreign countries are taxed at a reduced rate or are exempt from U.S. income taxes on certain items of income they receive from sources within the U.S. These reduced rates and exemptions vary among countries as to specific items of income. Very often, income received by students and scholars of these foreign countries, who are studying in the United States, are exempt from U.S. income tax.

The following countries have tax treaties or agreements with the United States: Antilles, Aruba, Australia, Austria, Barbados, Belgium, Canada, Cyprus, Denmark, Egypt, Finland, France, Germany, Greece, Hungary, Iceland, Ireland, Italy, Jamaica, Japan, Luxembourg, Malta, Morocco, the Netherlands, New Zealand, Norway, Pakistan, People's Republic of China, the Philippines, Poland, Republic of Korea, Romania, Sweden, Switzerland, Trinidad, Tobago, U.S.S.R., and the United Kingdom.

The IRS publishes information about the contents of these tax treaties. If you have questions regarding taxation, it is probably best to consult the local office of the IRS or an accountant to advise you.

When to File Your Income Tax Return

Every year, April 15 is the deadline for filing a return on the income earned during the preceding calendar year.

Sometime during January each year, your employer will send you a "W-2 Form", showing the amount you have earned during the preceding year and the amount of federal and state income tax that has been withheld. The W-2 Form is used in preparing your income tax return. The amount withheld often exceeds the amount you would be required to pay, so failure to file a tax return may result in a financial loss for you. You must file a return in order to receive a refund.

After leaving the United States, you can get a tax return form from the nearest U.S. consul for use in filing your taxes for the calendar year during which you left the United States. These forms become available in the January following your departure.

Choosing the Appropriate Tax Form

In order to choose the federal tax form that is appropriate for you, you must know whether you are classified as a "resident alien for tax purposes" or a "non-resident alien for tax purposes". In general, foreign students and scholars are classified as non-residents for tax purposes. Non-residents use an income tax form called Form 1040 NR.

Where to Get Tax Forms

Tax forms and instructions are usually available in bank lobbies and at IRS offices, and are available by telephone request (see "Getting Assistance" below). If you have previously filed an income tax return, a new one will be mailed to you in the following year.

Documentation

It is a very good idea to keep complete records of your financial transactions. Without good records, completing your income tax returns can be difficult. If you seek assistance from someone else in preparing your income tax returns, that person will need thorough records of your income and expenditures. Always keep a copy of any income tax form you submit, with all supporting records.

Getting Assistance in Filing Income Tax Returns

The IRS is responsible for collecting income taxes. You may address questions to or request forms from the IRS by calling 1-800-424-1040. The call is toll free.

There are a number of businesses which, for a fee, will assist taxpayers in preparing their income tax returns. You can find them in the yellow pages under "Tax Return Preparation".

Income tax laws and procedures are complex and ever-changing. Only a trained person whose business it is to remain up-to-date concerning those laws and procedures can help you.

SOCIAL SECURITY

"Social Security" is the U.S. government's social insurance plan. It is intended to benefit retired people and certain people who are injured, disabled, or left without adequate means of financial support. It is financed by means of withholdings from employees' pay and employers' contributions. Virtually all U.S. citizens have a "Social Security number" which designates their account with the Social Security Administration (SSA).

Social Security Tax

In general, people who are in F-1, M-1, or J-1 status and who are working legally are not required to pay into the Social Security fund (FICA). However, FICA regulations are currently undergoing revision and reinterpretation, and there may be situations in which FICA would be withheld from the paycheck of a person in F-1, M-1, or J-1 status. In any case, F-1, M-1, and J-1 visa holders would not be responsible for FICA taxes if their work falls into any of these categories:

- Services performed by an enrolled student for the school he/she regularly attends;

- Services performed for state or local government, unless an agreement with the federal government is involved;

- Services performed for a foreign government; or

- Services performed for an international organization.

If social security income tax was withheld in error from the pay received by an F, M, or J student, you may contact the employer who withheld the tax for reimbursement. If you are unable to obtain a refund from the employer, a claim for the refund may be filed with the IRS. The local office of the IRS should be contacted for further instructions on how to get a refund.

Obtaining a Social Security Number

If you are employed in the United States, you will need a Social Security number even if your pay is exempt from Social Security withholding. Some colleges and universities use a student's Social Security number as student identification numbers. To get a Social Security number, take your passport and Form I-94 to the office of the Social Security Administration near where you live. The application form is brief and simple. The passport is needed to prove your identity.

CHAPTER THIRTEEN

Getting Settled — Making a Home in the USA

Some psychologists believe that the single most important factor being a successful college student is having a comfortable and workable living arrangement. Some colleges and universities have on-campus housing facilities (often called dormitories or "dorms") owned and managed by the institution. Others provide extensive assistance to foreign students in obtaining comfortable living situations, often through the foreign students office or through a special housing office. Some educational institutions do not have the resources to assist foreign students with housing, and so you must fend for yourself, using other students and new friends or family to assist you.

Once you find housing, you will need to begin organizing your day to day life so that your experience at home enhances, rather than interferes with, your education and social life in college. For many students, college is their first experience living away from home, and for foreign students in particular, given the difficulty in learning the ways of a new culture, even the simplest activity, such as purchasing food, can be traumatic.

In this Chapter, we provide an overview of the types of housing commonly available to the foreign student, plus hints on shopping.

HOUSING

Rooms

A "room" has facilities for sleeping and studying. It may be in a private house or in a "rooming house", where there are many sleeping-studying rooms. In either case, bathrooms are usually shared with other residents. There may or may not be "kitchen privileges", meaning access to cooking facilities. Rents vary from city to city.

Apartments

An apartment is a complete living unit, with no facilities other than laundry machines that must be shared with other residents in the apartment building. An "efficiency apartment" has two rooms: a bathroom and another large room that serves as kitchen, bedroom, and living room. It is suitable for one or perhaps two people. There are also one-, two- and three-bedroom apartments. "Unfurnished apartments" have only a refrigerator, stove and window

coverings, and the renter must acquire all other furniture that is needed. A "furnished apartment" includes all furniture, but not linens (towels, sheets, etc.) or cooking and eating utensils. Since unfurnished apartments cost less and inexpensive second-hand (i.e., used) furniture is easy to buy and sell, people who will be in the United States for at least one year find it cheaper to rent an unfurnished apartment and buy used furnishings for it. A furnished apartment costs more, but eliminates the need to buy furniture. As a renter or "tenant" you will usually have to pay for your own utilities (i.e., electricity, gas, water, and telephone), although the monthly rent may include some of these. The landlord or manager can explain what you must do to begin utility services, that is, to get electricity and gas to your apartment.

Houses

Visiting foreign student and scholars who are here with their families may want to rent an entire house. Sometimes a group of students will join together to rent a house as well. Houses may be furnished or unfurnished. Houses for rent are usually located through real estate agents or through personal contacts with landlords or with renters who are vacating a house.

The Lease

A lease is a written agreement between a tenant and landlord, describing the rights and responsibilities of each. It is a binding legal document that, among other things, makes the tenant responsible for minimal care of the rented property and for the monthly rent of a stated amount for a stated period of time. It specifies the landlord's responsibilities for maintenance and repair of the housing unit. A lease may or may not contain provisions concerning its early termination. Students who are unsure how long they will be staying in an apartment will want to avoid signing a lease that binds them too long.

When you sign a lease, you will usually have to pay a "damage deposit" or a "security deposit" which may amount to as much as two months' rent. The landlord is supposed to return the deposit to you after you leave the apartment if you have paid your rent, left the apartment clean and undamaged, and have not been evicted. If the landlord does not return all of your deposit, he or she should give you a written statement explaining why some or all of the deposit was withheld. Most cities have associations which help tenants who have disputes with landlords about unreturned damage deposits.

What should one look for in a lease? First of all, duration. Make sure you can keep the room or apartment as long as you wish, but that the lease is not binding for a time period longer than you anticipate needing the housing. See whether it is renewable by the month or the year. See whether you can "break" the lease with a month or two months' notice to the landlord. In the absence of such a provision, you may have to pay rent until the end of the period covered by the lease even if you move out and live elsewhere. Or, if the lease allows it, you may be able to "sublet" your room or apartment. That means, essentially, that you find another tenant to rent your apartment in your absence.

Secondly, see what utilities you are responsible for. Ask the landlord or a current tenant what average utility costs are, because utility costs must be added to rent in determining your monthly housing cost.

Most cities have housing codes which guarantee minimal living standards in rented rooms and apartments. Landlords are required to provide adequate winter heating and regular insect control. If you make any special agreements with the landlord concerning repairs or alterations, make sure those agreements are written into the lease, signed, and dated. (Americans consider it essential to have important agreements written down and signed.)

Lastly, bear in mind that a lease may contain many restrictions and exclusions. Common ones apply to children and pet animals.

Renting Without a Lease

Some landlords do not require you to sign a lease. One of the things a lease does is to prevent the landlord from raising the rent for the duration of the lease. According to most standard leases, the landlord must also maintain the unit and be responsible for any repairs on structural elements or appliances provided (this includes plumbing, heating equipment, appliances, and so forth). Without a lease, the tenant does not have these guarantees, although the landlord must meet certain "habitability standards" even if the lease is not written. The landlord, like the tenant, can end a verbal rental agreement by providing 30 days' written notice to the tenant.

Utilities

Once you have your housing, you may need to contact services which provide utilities such as gas, electricity, and water. Ask your landlord which services are included in the rental costs.

Renter's Insurance

Prudent tenants are encouraged to purchase "renter's insurance" (which might also be called "homeowner's insurance") to protect against losses caused by fire, theft, or vandalism. This kind of insurance covers personal belongings in your room or apartment, and in your car if you have one. It also covers damages for which you would be legally liable if a fire or other accident that was your responsibility damaged the building in which you rent and/or the property of other renters in your building. The cost of renter's insurance varies depending on the value of your personal possessions, but is relatively low. When buying insurance, it is considered wise to get rate information from two or three different insurance agents. You can find agents' names and telephone numbers in the telephone directory yellow pages under "Insurance".

BUYING THINGS

Most items can be purchased from a variety of stores. Since prices and quality vary, it is helpful to become acquainted with those stores that are most convenient and economical. Such information is available from people who have lived in your city, from advertisements in newspapers, and from the "yellow pages" section of the telephone directory. You can ask a store employee whatever questions you wish about a product without having to buy anything.

Prices in most stores are fixed. A shopper does not usually "bargain" for a lower price with the store employee, except in the case of automobiles and large appliances although the practice of "bargaining" for electronic goods and other smaller items is growing. Many stores operate on a "self-service" basis. In these stores, the shopper uses one of the baskets or carts provided and selects the merchandise desired. The merchandise is then taken to the cashier, who totals the amount of the purchase and adds the appropriate sales tax.

When you buy something other than food, it is advisable to keep the receipt you get when you pay for the item. You will need the receipt if the item is defective or unsatisfactory and you need to return it to the store where you bought it. The receipt also proves you made the purchase.

Sales Taxes

A sales tax is added to the cost of some purchases in some states and cities. Income generated from sales taxes is used to support various state- and city-run programs, such as highway maintenance, public education, and law enforcement. So the final price of an item is not the ticketed price, but that price plus the relevant sales tax.

Food

There are three general kinds of food stores: "supermarkets", "neighborhood stores", and "convenience stores". A supermarket is a large store which sells not only groceries but also paper goods, kitchen supplies, and health and beauty aids. Neighborhood stores and convenience stores are smaller, have far fewer non-food items, usually have longer hours of business, and charge somewhat higher prices. Convenience stores usually sell gasoline and some automobile supplies as well as a limited range of foods. Most people do nearly all their food shopping at the supermarket most convenient for them, and go to neighborhood stores or convenience stores only to buy one or two items needed quickly.

Foods from your country may not be available in the supermarket, but they may be available from a specialty food store. Ask other students here from your country where they buy such foods.

Clothing

Clothing is for sale in clothing stores (often separate stores for men's and women's clothing), department stores (which have "departments" for selling a variety of merchandise, including clothing, hardware, appliances, furniture, fabric and sewing supplies, kitchen utensils, shoes, books, records, and toys) and at second-hand stores such as the Goodwill Industries (which sell used merchandise at low prices).

Furniture

Buying furniture for a new apartment can be a large undertaking, so this section includes extensive information on places to look for less expensive furniture. Furniture stores, department stores, and second-hand stores all sell furniture. In addition, used furniture is often available from private individuals who have "garage sales" at their homes or who advertise the items they wish to sell in the classified section of the newspaper.

Discount Furniture

 Discount furniture is new furniture that is sold at a reduced price because it was damaged in shipping, or because it represents the remnants of a style or model of furniture that is no longer being produced, or for some other similar reason. It is usually higher priced and better quality than used furniture. Some local furniture dealers may stock discount furniture. Furniture that is new but not yet painted (unfinished) can be purchased in many discount stores.

Health Products

"Drug stores" or pharmacies sell not only medicines and toiletries (i.e., soap, toothpaste, shaving cream, deodorant, shampoo, etc.), but also small household goods, stationery, magazines, and newspapers.

Household Goods

Items such as small appliances, kitchen utensils, and cleaning equipment are available at many places, including department stores, drug stores, hardware stores, second-hand stores, and from private individuals selling through the want ads.

CHAPTER FOURTEEN

Money Management

Many foreign students, like large numbers of U.S. students, live on limited budgets. It is important to be cautious about spending money until you are accustomed to the value of the dollar and thoroughly understand how much your essential living expenses will cost. In thinking about the value of the dollar, it helps to realize that the minimum wage in the United States in 1992 was $4.25 per hour. At that rate, it would take nearly four hours of work to buy a $15 book, and about twelve hours of work to buy a $50 pair of shoes.

In this Chapter, we provide useful information regarding the spending and saving of your money including how to open a bank account.

UNITED STATES CURRENCY

Coins

U.S. coins come in two colors and six sizes. Smaller-sized coins are not always lower in value than larger coins.

- The **penny or cent**, worth 1 cent, is the only copper-colored coin.

- The **nickel**, worth 5 cents, is silver-colored and larger than a penny.

- The **dime**, worth 10 cents, is silver-colored and is the smallest U.S. coin.

- The **quarter**, worth 25 cents, is silver in color and is larger than the nickel.

- The **half-dollar**, or 50-cent-piece, is silver in color and larger than the quarter, and not in common use.

The silver dollar comes in two forms, neither of which is seen very often in circulation. The Susan B. Anthony silver dollar is about the size of a quarter; the older silver dollar is the largest U.S. coin.

Paper Money

All U.S. paper money is the same size and color. Denominations include $1 (commonly called a "buck"), $5, $10, $20, $50, $100 and larger amounts. Paper money for amounts over $100 is not usually seen in public circulation.

OPENING A BANK ACCOUNT

To open any kind of bank account, go to the bank of your choice and tell the receptionist that you would like to open an account. Two people can initiate a "joint account" which either or both of them can use.

Checking Account
(called a "current account" in many countries)

It is very important to keep a running balance of your account each time you write a check. A charge is levied each time you "overdraw" your account, that is, each time you write a check which is not covered by the amount you have deposited in your account.

Most people pay their bills by means of personal checks, sometimes delivered personally but usually sent through the mail. (Cash should never be sent in the mail.) Sending checks through the mail is the most convenient way to pay your bills. Your canceled checks, returned to you monthly or held for safekeeping at your bank after they have been cashed by the persons to whom you wrote them, are legal receipts for payments you have made. You or your bank should therefore retain all canceled checks which were used to pay bills.

Personalized Checks

Nearly all banking customers use personalized checks. Personalized checks have your name, address, and Social Security number or other information you choose printed on them. Usually you must pay a few dollars for your supply of personalized checks, so it is wise to wait until you have an address, Social Security number, and phone number before you have your checks printed. In the meantime, the bank will issue you a temporary supply of blank checks.

Savings Account

A savings account earns interest at relatively low rates. If you have several hundreds of dollars above your routine living expenses, a savings account is a safe way to invest it. You can withdraw any amount from a regular (or "passbook") savings account whenever it is necessary. If you have a savings and a checking account in the same bank, you can telephone and ask the bank to transfer funds from your savings to your checking account. Federal regulations limit the number of automatic transfers from savings to no more than three per month or statement cycle.

Banks also offer "savings certificates" and "money market certificates" which require specified minimum deposits and earn higher rates of interest than regular savings accounts, but which must remain on deposit for designated periods of time. A savings certificate or money market certificate is a prudent investment if you are certain that you will not need the money until the designated time period has elapsed (which can be 90 days, six months, one year, or more). This is usually called a "certificate of deposit" or "CD".

Automatic Teller Machines (ATMs)

The automatic teller is a computerized device through which bank customers can make deposits or withdrawals at any time of the day, any day of the week. To operate an ATM, the customer needs a particular plastic card (called an "instant access card") and a personal identification number (or "PIN") that the bank provides, although a few banks will let you select one. Instructions for operating the automatic teller are given on the machine itself. Unlike some other banking systems, in the United States you may withdraw money from any bank that belongs to a system, such as CIRRUS or NYCE, anywhere in the country.

Automatic tellers are located at banks and at some other locations, including supermarkets, shopping centers, residence halls, and hospitals.

Electronic Funds Transfer

The electronic funds transfer is a method of transferring money from one bank to another. It can also be used to pay bills and deposit checks without physically handling the money. Bills can be paid automatically each month by asking your bank to send money to certain companies to whom you owe money. This is a common method of paying utility bills. If you work, your check can be automatically deposited in your account in the same way. This saves time, stamps, and envelopes. It also makes sure your bills are never late. If you are interested in electronic funds transfer, contact your bank.

Traveler's Checks

Traveler's checks provide a safe way to carry money when traveling in the United States and abroad. They can be replaced if they are lost, and they are more easily accepted by businesses away from your own area of residence. Banks and credit unions sell traveler's checks for a small fee.

Tuesday

October
1

CHAPTER FIFTEEN

Day to Day Living

In this Chapter, we provide insights on coping with a variety of day to day concerns including medical care and insurance, telephone and mail services, advice for people with children, tips on safety and security and the role of the police. We also provide a list of major holidays in the United States.

MEDICAL CARE AND INSURANCE

The United States is the only major industrialized nation in the world, apart from South Africa, which does not have a national health care plan. This means that people living in the United States must purchase — either at their own expense or through a plan sponsored by their employer, union or other organization — a medical insurance plan. Since the cost of medical care and emergency health needs are not met by the U.S. government, they must be paid for by the individual.

With the exception of J-1 exchange visitors (whose sponsors are required to provide limited insurance), foreign students are not required by the Immigration and

Naturalization Service (INS) to have medical insurance. However, some schools do require foreign students to purchase medical insurance before they register or attend the school. Some schools have a mandatory medical insurance plan which must be purchased at the time of registration for classes. Other schools require the student to show proof of purchase of a medical insurance plan. The National Association of Foreign Student Advisors (NAFSA) has several plans available to foreign students in the United States which they recommend. Information on these plans can be obtained from your foreign student advisor.

Where a U.S. school maintains its own health care facilities, foreign students are generally allowed to participate and use the facilities.

If you have an emergency medical problem, you can be treated in an emergency room of a hospital. Federal U.S. laws require that both public and private hospitals provide services to anyone needing emergency medical care regardless of whether that person is eligible for Medicaid (a government funded medical program which pays for all or part of medical expenses for individuals of low income) or has private funds to pay for the services.

HIV AND AIDS

If you are sexually active, you should protect yourself from Human Immune Deficiency Virus infection, known as "HIV". This is the virus which ultimately leads to Acquired Immune Deficiency Syndrome, referred to as "AIDS". Any person, regardless of sexual preference or race, can become infected with HIV. HIV can be transmitted:

- by sexual contact (including unprotected sexual intercourse and oral-genital contact) that entails exposure to the partner's bodily fluids (semen and lubricating fluids produced during sexual excitation),

- by direct exposure to infected blood, as happens, for example, when intravenous drug users share needles, or

- from an HIV infected woman to her fetus during pregnancy or childbirth, or, possibly, to her infant during breast feeding.

There is NO risk of transmitting HIV by sharing any of the following with a person who is infected with HIV:

- a bathroom,

- a glass or eating utensils,

- a swimming pool or recreational facilities, or

- books.

Nor is HIV transmitted by coughing or sneezing, and it is safe to hold hands or otherwise touch an infected person. In other words, there is no risk of becoming infected by what health professionals call "casual contact" with an infected person. HIV is transmitted only through semen, vaginal fluids, or blood. You cannot tell if a person is infected with HIV by looking at them.

Medical facilities in the United States are required by law to protect patients and health care workers from the risk of HIV. It is considered safe to accept medical treatment from a hospital in the United States. Needles are discarded after one use, blood is screened and workers are required to wear protective clothing.

You can protect yourself from AIDS by not sharing needles with anyone. This includes needles used not just for injecting drugs, but also needles used for acupuncture, ear-piercing, and tattooing. If you engage in sexual activity with another person, always use a condom and avoid contact between mucous membranes and semen, vaginal secretions, and blood.

If you have questions about HIV or AIDS, contact your doctor.

CHILDREN

Schools

- **Pre-Schools and Day-Care Centers** (for children younger than five, the age at which a child begins kindergarten). You will find a number of pre-schools listed in the yellow pages of the telephone directory. These schools vary considerably with respect to cost, philosophy of instruction, pupil-teacher ratio, and schedule. Generally, a pre-school has shorter sessions and emphasizes educational activity. By contrast, day-care facilities have longer hours and are intended to be places where children can receive care while their parents are otherwise occupied.

- **Public Schools** (for children five and older). Public schools in the United States provide free education for children between the ages of 5 and 18. If your child is entering school for the first time, you will need a birth certificate or other indication of your child's age. If your child has previously attended school, you will need a transcript of grades or some other document indicating the grade level at which your child should be placed. Students do not need to speak English in order to enter the public schools in most cities.

- **Private Schools.** The families of children attending private schools must pay tuition. Costs vary, depending on the age or grade and on the particular school. Like public schools, private schools are open to any student, regardless of religious affiliation.

SAFETY AND SECURITY

Movies and television, and news reports from the United States that appear abroad, may convey the impression that serious crime is widespread, not just in major cities but all over the country. This impression is not well founded. The rates of crime and violence are higher in some parts of the United States than others. It is therefore wise to take certain precautions to protect yourself and your property. Here are some specific suggestions:

Personal Safety

Keep your doors locked even when you are at home. If someone knocks at your door or rings your doorbell, do not open the door until you have asked who is there. You are not required to open the door simply because someone knocks. If it is someone claiming to be an official, ask to see some identification.

Leave both an outside and an inside light on if you will be away from your room or apartment after dark.

Follow the guidelines in the front of the telephone book if you receive obscene or threatening telephone calls.

Women are advised to be particularly cautious. Avoid walking alone at night, especially in areas that are not well lighted. Walk with a companion, or find a ride in a bus or car. If you must walk, vary your route.

REMEMBER: The Police Department operates a special phone number for emergency use only. Dial 911 in case of an emergency. (Be sure to check whether "911" exists in your area.)

Identification Documents

In many countries the law requires every person to carry an identity card at all times. There is no such requirement in the United States. There is no national identity card.

An identification document of some kind is often needed, though, especially to cash checks or to make purchases with checks. Most colleges and universities issue student identification cards that can be used for this purpose.

A passport can also be offered as proof of identity. (Passports are not familiar to all clerks.) Most Americans use a driver's license as an ID card.

CARS AND BICYCLES

Driver's License

With few exception, anyone living in the United States and driving a car here must have a driver's license. You may drive legally in most states if you have a current International Driver's License (issued for one year only) and your home country driver's license in your possession while you drive. It is advisable, however, to obtain a state license even if your international license is still valid.

It is very important to learn and follow traffic regulations. Regulations concerning driving speed, turning, and parking are used to control automobile (and bicycle) traffic in the United States.

Most people generally adhere to those regulations, and the regulations are enforced by the police. Violations of traffic regulations are punished by fines, jail sentences, and/or loss of driving privileges. Cars which are parked in violation of regulations may be towed away, and the owner required to pay a fine, towing costs, and storage costs.

When you buy a car the "certificate of ownership" or "certificate of title" must be transferred to you from the previous owner, and you must register it.

It is essential to have at least liability insurance if you have a car, since you are financially responsible if you cause your car to injure another person or damage someone else's property.

Automobile Insurance. There are several types of automobile insurance:

- **Liability insurance** is the most basic type. It protects you if your car kills or injures someone else, or damages someone else's property. You are considered legally liable if a car you own (whether you or someone else is driving it) causes injury or death to another person or damage to someone else's property, unless the accident is clearly not the fault of the person driving your car. If you are legally liable for injuries, death, or damages resulting from an automobile accident, you could face payments of tens of thousands of dollars. If you do not have liability insurance to help pay those costs, you will have to pay them yourself. This is why you will want to have liability insurance, even if your car itself is not very valuable.

- **Collision insurance** protects your car in case of collision with another car.

- **Comprehensive insurance** covers losses caused by storms, thieves, and vandals.

Buying Car Insurance

In the yellow pages of the telephone directory you will find a long list of insurance agents under the heading "Insurance". Unless a friend can recommend a reliable agent to you, you should talk to at least two agents about your insurance needs. The amount of insurance you buy for your car should depend on its value. Insurance rates vary from company to company, and they depend also on the value of the car, the amount it is driven, the age of the drivers, the past driving records of the drivers, and even the car's color.

BICYCLES

Buying a Bicycle

Bicycling is popular as a sport and means of transportation in the United States. So, many of the bicycles for sale here are very elaborate ten-speed racing models or rugged "all-terrain" bicycles. If you are using your bicycle for transportation only, you may not need such expensive models.

Bicycle Registration

You do not need to license a bicycle in most cities. However, you may wish to have your bicycle's serial number registered at the Police Department. In some cities, having the serial number registered can help the police recover your bicycle if it is stolen.

Bicycle Theft

It is important to lock your bicycle securely whenever you leave it. Ask the person who sells you the bicycle to recommend an effective lock for it. In some cities, bike shop staff recommend never leaving your bike alone, even when locked.

Bicycle Safety

When you are riding your bicycle on a street or road, you must obey the same rules and traffic signs as a motorist. You can be ticketed by police and be required to pay a fine for violating traffic regulations with a bicycle, just as you can for violating them with a car. There are hand signals you should use to let motorists know when you plan to make a turn. Putting your left arm straight out from your side signals a left turn. Bending the left arm upwards at the elbow indicates a right turn. If you are riding your bicycle before sunrise or after sunset, you must have a headlight and rear light or reflector. It is also a good idea to wear light-colored or reflective clothing especially when riding at night, and a protective helmet.

POLICE AND LAW ENFORCEMENT

Local Police

The police have different roles in different countries. The primary role of the police is to investigate crimes and arrest the alleged perpetrator (the person who committed the crime). Another common police activity is giving parking tickets to people who have parked their cars in illegal places or have parked "overtime" in metered parking places. The police expect residents to ask their help with such matters as lost or stolen property, noisy neighbors, and "suspicious activity" they witness in their neighborhoods.

Federal Law Enforcement Agencies

The federal law enforcement agency responsible for enforcing the immigration laws is the Immigration and Naturalization Service (INS). No other agency shares responsibility for acting in cases where aliens might have violated the terms of their immigration status.

Another federal law-enforcement agency, the Federal Bureau of Investigation (FBI), has responsibilities that sometimes (not often) lead their agents to wish to question foreign students and scholars. Foreign students and scholars are not required to answer any questions addressed to them by an FBI agent unless the agent has obtained a court order (called a "subpoena") mandating a reply. If an FBI agent asks you to answer some questions and does not have a subpoena you can, if you wish, simply say that you prefer not to answer any questions. Doing so will not affect your immigration status. If you are contacted by the FBI and are uncertain how to respond, you may want to consult a foreign student advisor or attorney

HOLIDAYS IN THE UNITED STATES

General Information

The United States has adopted legislation which moved the celebration of several holidays to the Monday nearest the date of the event the holiday commemorated. The purpose of this legislation was to create as many "three-day weekends" (i.e., Saturday-Sunday-Monday) as possible.

Four principal national holidays — New Year's Day, Independence Day, Thanksgiving, and Christmas — were not subjects of the date-changing legislation. They are still celebrated on the same day each year. Another principal holiday, Labor Day, has traditionally been on Monday. Many businesses and all government offices close in observance of these holidays.

Of the holidays on the following list, not all are celebrated throughout the United States and not all are celebrated by everyone. Some are holidays only for members of certain religions; others are for particular groups, such as lovers or children.

Holiday Calendar

The following list indicates which are legal holidays (when government offices are closed) and which are business holidays (when many businesses, except some drugstores, service stations, and food stores) are closed.

NEW YEAR'S DAY (January 1). Celebration of New Year's Day usually occurs the night before, on "New Year's Eve", when it is common for groups of people to have a party to celebrate the coming of the new year. Alcoholic beverages are usually consumed at these parties. It is customary to make loud noises at midnight, when the new year officially arrives; embracing or kissing others at the part at midnight is not unusual. A legal and business holiday.

MARTIN LUTHER KING'S BIRTHDAY (January 15, but celebrated the third Monday in January). A legal holiday in some states, but not all, this holiday commemorates the civil rights leader.

ABRAHAM LINCOLN'S BIRTHDAY (February 12 or nearest Monday). See President's Day.

ST. VALENTINE'S DAY (February 14). A day for lovers to exchange cards and/or gifts. Children in primary school usually exchange "valentine cards" with their classmates.

GEORGE WASHINGTON'S BIRTHDAY (February 22 or nearest Monday). Commemorates the birthday of the first President of the United States.

PRESIDENT'S DAY (third Monday in February). Commemorates Lincoln's and Washington's birthdays. A legal holiday.

ASH WEDNESDAY (date varies). Marks the beginning of the 40-day period of Lent, a period of penitence and fasting in some Christian denominations. On Ash Wednesday, some Christians attend a church service during which small ash marks are placed on their foreheads to symbolize our ultimate return to dust.

ST. PATRICK'S DAY (March 17). A day dedicated to the patron saint of Ireland. Many people wear something green on this day.

EASTER SUNDAY (date varies sometime in March or April). Christians celebrate the resurrection of Jesus. For children, baskets of candy and dyed, hard-boiled eggs are hidden by a mythical "Easter Rabbit" or "Easter Bunny". The children playfully search for the hidden eggs.

MOTHER'S DAY (the second Sunday in May). Gifts, cards, and/or special attention are given to mothers and grandmothers.

MEMORIAL DAY (May 30 or the nearest Monday). A legal and business holiday when homage is paid to U.S. soldiers who have died in wars.

FATHER'S DAY (the third Sunday in June). Gifts, cards, and/or special attention are given to fathers and grandfathers.

INDEPENDENCE DAY, usually termed "the Fourth of July" (July 4). Parades, fireworks (which are now illegal in most states), and flags to celebrate the signing of the U.S. Declaration of Independence from Great Britain. A legal and business holiday.

LABOR DAY (the first Monday of September). A legal and business holiday noting the importance of labor and labor organizations.

ROSH HASHANAH is the Jewish New Year and YOM KIPPUR the Jewish Day of Atonement (both celebrated on varying dates in September or October).

COLUMBUS DAY (October 12 or nearest Monday). Commemorates the landing of Italian explorer Christopher Columbus on the shores of North America. A legal holiday, but not a business one.

HALLOWEEN (October 31). A children's holiday, associated with carving faces on pumpkins called "jack-o'lanterns" and making witches, cats, and ghosts for decorations. Children often go to parties in costumes or go "trick or treating". "Trick or treating" means putting on a costume and going door-to-door in a neighborhood saying "trick or treat", and being given a piece of candy or fruit by the occupant of the house or apartment. Young children should be accompanied by an adult when trick or treating.

ELECTION DAY (the first Tuesday in November). Not a legal or business holiday, but people may leave work briefly in order to vote in municipal, county, state, and/or national elections.

VETERANS' DAY (November 11) A legal holiday, honoring veterans of armed service.

THANKSGIVING DAY (fourth Thursday in November). A harvest celebration, stemming from harvest-time festivities in the original American colonies. A legal and business holiday when, traditionally, families gather and have a large meal that includes turkey and pumpkin pie.

HANUKKAH (late November or early December). An eight-day Jewish holiday marking the rededication of the Second Temple in Jerusalem.

CHRISTMAS (December 25). Many see this as the major U.S. holiday. It began as a Christian celebration of the birth of Jesus, but is now a widely celebrated day of feasting and gift-giving. Preparations, including gift-buying and decoration of homes and public places, begin as early as Thanksgiving. "Santa Claus", a mythical figure, is said to visit the homes of children on the night of December 24 and leave gifts for them while they sleep.

GLOSSARY

Advance Parole

Advance parole is permission to return to the United States obtained from the Immigration and Naturalization Service (INS) prior to an individual's departure. It is necessary when a person is otherwise ineligible for reentry, such as where the person's visa has expired. It is available only in exceptional circumstances.

Advisory Opinion

The term "advisory opinion" in this Handbook is used to describe the process of seeking review by the U.S. Department of State of a denial of a nonimmigrant visa by a U.S. consular officer.

Affidavit

An affidavit is a sworn statement. In the United States, an affidavit is commonly signed in front of a notary public, who then puts his or her own stamp or seal on the document and signs under the signature of the person making the affidavit. Different countries have their own procedures regarding the certification of sworn documents. A person outside of the United States will sometimes sign an affidavit in front of a consular officer.

Affidavit of Support

An affidavit of support is a sworn statement by one individual indicating that he or she has the capability and willingness to support another individual. It is commonly used to support applications for student visas and for permanent residence. When an affidavit of support is submitted on behalf of an individual, the person who signs the affidavit is promising to support the individual if necessary, but there is no legal obligation. Therefore, if the person who benefits from the affidavit of support should incur a substantial debt, the person who signs the affidavit would not be responsible for that debt.

Alien

An alien is an individual who is not a United States citizen. Many people do not like the term alien because it is used commonly to describe visitors from "outer space". Since the immigration and nationality laws use the term alien to describe any person who is not a United States citizen, we occasionally use the term in this Handbook.

Asylum

An individual may apply for asylum in the United States if he or she is in the United States and believes that he or she will be persecuted because of race, religion, national origin, political opinion, or membership in a social group if forced to return to his or her country of nationality. A person granted asylum may reside here until conditions in the home country allow him or her to return. A person granted asylum may eventually apply for permanent residence.

Conditional Resident (Marriage and Investor)

The U.S. immigration laws provide two situations where an individual seeking to become a lawful permanent resident must go through a conditional resident stage. A conditional resident has all the rights and benefits of a permanent resident -- with the exception that twenty-one months after they have entered conditional resident status, they have 90 days to apply to the Immigration and Naturalization Service (INS) to have the condition removed. A person is a conditional resident if (1) he or she became a permanent resident based on marriage to a permanent resident or a U.S. citizen and obtained lawful permanent resident status within two years of that marriage or (2) he or she became a permanent resident based on an investment of money in the United States under the employment creation visa program.

Consul, Consulate

A consulate is an office of the United States government in a foreign country. It is often located at a U.S. Embassy. In some large populated countries, there may be several consulates. Most consulates issue visas and provide information for an individual who would like to come temporarily or permanently to the United States. A consul is an officer in charge of a consulate. In most cases, a consul will not deal directly with an individual applying for a nonimmigrant or immigrant visa. That duty will be delegated to a vice consul or other employee of the consulate.

Consular Officer

"Consular officer" is used in this Handbook as referring to any official working in a United States consulate who has the authority to issue a nonimmigrant visa or immigrant visa.

Consular Processing

Consular processing refers to applying for a nonimmigrant or immigrant visa at an U.S. consulate.

Co-op Program

A cooperative (or "co-op") or internship program refers to an employment program for students. Commonly, a private institution will develop a program in coordination with a college or university which will allow students to work for the commercial institution receiving college credit. Some of these programs are mandatory requirements for graduation while others are voluntary. Where they are mandatory, a foreign student may qualify for curricular practical training.

Deportation

Deportation is the process of removing an individual from the United States because he or she violated his or her immigration status. Contrary to what many people think, relatively few individuals unlawfully in the United States are forced to leave against their will.

Designated School Official (DSO) & Foreign Student Advisor (FSA)

At every college and university accredited by the Immigration and Naturalization Service (INS) to accept foreign students and issue Form I-20, there must be a designated school official (or "DSO") — sometimes called a foreign student advisor (or "FSA") — who is responsible for implementing immigration laws and regulations on behalf of the college or university. In larger educational institutions, an individual has this responsibility full-time. In some institutions, the registrar, the admissions officer, or some other school official may have this authority. The terms "foreign student advisor" and "designated school official" are often used interchangeably.

Duration of Status (D/S)

"Duration of status" or "D/S" refers to a designation given to F-1 students upon entry to the United States, indicating that they may remain in the United States throughout their program of study, plus any post-completion practical training, plus 60 days — so long as they comply with the rules and regulations that apply to F-1 students. (See also Form I-94, Arrival/Departure Record.)

Employment Authorization Document (EAD)

Some individuals who are authorized to work in the United States, such as F-1 students engaged in post-completion practical training, must obtain an employment authorization document or "EAD" from the Immigration and Naturalization Service (INS). Not every individual authorized to work in the United States is required to have an EAD.

Foreign Student Advisor (FSA) or International Student Advisor.
See Designated School Official, above.

Form I-94, Arrival/Departure Record

Form I-94 is issued to you at the port of entry and shows that you have been lawfully admitted to the United States. The Form I-94 is usually stapled onto the United States visa page of your passport. It contains an eleven-digit identifying number that the Immigration and Naturalization Service (INS) uses to keep track of your arrival and departure from the United States.

There may be a date written in the upper right-hand corner of your Form I-94. You are required by the INS to leave the United States by that date or apply to extend your stay. If there is no date, but rather the inscription "D/S" (duration of status), you are admitted for the length of your program of study as indicated on your Form I-20 ID, plus any period of post-completion of study practical training, plus 60 days. If you graduate before the completion date indicated on your Form I-20 ID, you are considered to have completed your program of study, and your Form I-20 ID is no longer valid.

Illegal Alien

The press and many individuals often refer to a foreign born person who is out of status as an "illegal alien". This is neither a helpful nor accurate term. In most cases, an individual out of status in the United States has broken no criminal laws. Further, people who may be considered out of status by the Immigration and Naturalization Service (INS) are eligible for relief under our immigration laws and will be allowed to remain in the United States. Also, while a person can do things which are illegal, the idea that a person can be illegal makes no sense and therefore is inherently pejorative.

Immigrant

An immigrant is an individual who is coming or has come to the United States to reside here for an indefinite period. A lawful immigrant or lawful permanent resident is an individual who has obtained permanent resident status. This individual is often referred to as holding a "green card", although the card that is used to identify a lawful permanent resident is no longer green. An immigrant can reside indefinitely in the United States, is eligible to work in most jobs with the exception of some government jobs, and eventually may become a U.S. citizen.

Immigration and Naturalization Service (INS)

The Immigration and Naturalization Service, referred to as the "INS", is the agency of the U.S. government responsible for enforcing our immigration laws. While the INS maintains offices abroad, the most important aspect of their work is the enforcement of U.S. immigration laws within the United States. They maintain the border patrol and the inspection stations at U.S. ports of entry, including land, sea, and air entry points. They are also responsible for adjudicating an individual's eligibility for many nonimmigrant statuses and permanent residence.

Labor Attestation

F-1 students may work in a job of their choosing after having been in F-1 status for one school year, provided the employer files with the U.S. Department of Labor what is called a "labor attestation". In this attestation, the employer must state that it has recruited for the job for six months and is offering the job at the prevailing wage.

Labor Certification

Many individuals seeking to become permanent residents based on an offer of employment are required to obtain a labor certification. Generally, a labor certification is certification by the U.S. Department of Labor that the job for which an individual is seeking permanent residence or some cases nonimmigrant status cannot be filled by a lawful U.S. worker and is being offered at the prevailing wage.

Labor Condition Application

An individual who has a four year college degree or higher (or the equivalent in education and training) may apply for employment authorization as an H-1B temporary professional worker. An employer petitioning on behalf of this individual must submit an application — called a labor condition application or "LCA" — to the U.S. Department of Labor indicating that the wage being offered to the foreign worker is the higher of the prevailing wage or the highest wage paid for that position on the job site and that notice of the job has been posted at the place of employment.

Motion to Reconsider

In this Handbook, we commonly describe situations where an application is made to the Immigration and Naturalization Service and that application is denied. The individual may ask to have his or her case reconsidered. This is not really an "appeal" of the decision, since the individual is going back to the organization that made the original decision and asking it to take a second look. When a motion to reconsider is made, it is important that the reason is clearly stated why the individual making the motion believes the first decision was wrong. In most cases where a case is denied because a crucial fact was not established to the satisfaction of the Immigration and Naturalization Service (INS), it is useful to submit supplementary documentation to augment the documentation already provided.

Nonimmigrant

A nonimmigrant is an individual who is coming to the United States or has come to the United States for a purpose which is limited. The limitations concern the activities the individual can engage in and the amount of time the individual is allowed to remain in the United States. Some visas, including all student visas, require that the individual establish that he or she is a nonimmigrant. That is, the alien presently intends to come to the United States for a limited purpose and for a limited period of time. A nonimmigrant may have in mind the possibility of becoming a permanent resident, provided he or she understands that the current status or entry is limited and he or she must abide by those limitations.

Passport

Your passport is your own government's permit for you to leave and re-enter your own country. Most passports contain an expiration date. In place of a passport, some students hold a Certificate of Identity (often called a "CI"), which is roughly equivalent to a passport. A valid passport or CI is normally required to obtain a U.S. visa and to enter the United States.

Permanent Resident

The term permanent resident refers to an individual who is authorized to live and work indefinitely in the United States. A permanent resident is referred to alternatively as a "lawful permanent resident", "LPR", or "green card holder". (Note, however, that the alien registration card is no longer green in color.) After three or five years, depending on the facts of an individual's case, a permanent resident may apply to become a U.S. citizen.

Petition

The term "petition" is used to describe the process used by an employer or relative to apply for a benefit on behalf of an alien. Petition also refers to the form that is actually filed on behalf of the employee or alien.

Practical Training: Pre-Completion, Post-Completion, and Curricular

Practical training refers to employment by a foreign student in field related to their area of study. It is employment which is recognized under our immigration laws and requires authorization from the foreign student advisor or designated school official. Practical training may be pre- or post-graduation. Where the employment is a requirement for a degree, it is called curricular practical training.

Practitioner

Other than your foreign student advisor or designated student officer (who can speak or write to the Immigration and Naturalization Service (INS) in an official capacity), the only individuals legally authorized to represent you before the INS are "practitioners" (attorneys) and accredited representatives. An attorney must be licensed by a state of the United States, the District of Columbia, or Puerto Rico. An accredited representative is an individual who is working for a not-for-profit organization who has been accredited by the Immigration and Naturalization Service (INS) to represent individuals at no or low cost.

Program Officer

A program officer is the designated school official (see Designated School Official, above) responsible for implementation of an exchange visitor program at a college or university. It may be the foreign student advisor or designated school official who is responsible for supervising an F-1 or M-1 student, or it might be a separate individual or individuals. The program officer has authority to grant employment authorization and assist in the applications for extensions of J-1 student status.

Registry

Registry is the process by which an individual who has continually resided in the United States since January 1, 1972 may apply for permanent residence.

Reinstatement of Status

Sometimes an individual who has failed to maintain status can be reinstated into a lawful status by applying to the Immigration and Naturalization Service (INS). Reinstatement is usually allowed only when the student fell out of status through no fault of his or her own.

Third Country Processing

Third country processing refers to the situation where an individual is applying for a nonimmigrant or immigrant visa in a country other than their country of last residence. It is called third country processing because it is in neither the United States nor the individual's country of residence but in a "third" country.

United States Information Agency (USIA)

The United States Information Agency (USIA) is located in Washington, D.C. and is responsible for implementing the J-1 exchange visitor program. Inquiries regarding J-1 status or the exchange visitor program can be made directly to the USIA at United States Information Agency, 301 Fourth Street, S.W., Washington, D.C. 20547.

Visa (Nonimmigrant)

A nonimmigrant visa is a stamp put in your passport by the U.S. consular officer to show you may enter the United States as a nonimmigrant. The visa indicates the latest date on which you can apply to enter this country. It does not show how long you can stay here. It also indicates the kind of visa you have in the case of students or scholars, usually F-1, M-1, or J-1. U.S. visas come in two formats. The traditional one is a red and blue stamp. The newer format is a computer-printed, adhesive-backed piece of paper that is placed on a page of the passport. Much of the information on the computer-printed visa is in code.

When you arrive at your "port of entry", the U.S. immigration inspector examines your passport, your visa, and your Certificate of Eligibility (if you have an F-1, M-1, or J-1 visa), and determines whether you are admissible to the United States.

A nonimmigrant visa may be a multiple entry visa which means it can be used for an unlimited number of entries into the United States, or it may be limited to a certain number of entries, even as few as one. The concept of "visa" which is a document used to enter the United States should not be confused with an individual's status. An individual may come to the United States using a visa such as a B-2 visitor's visa and then change his or her status to F-1 status which is student status. If that individual wishes to travel outside of the United States and then return to the United States, he or she will need to obtain a visa.

Waiver

On occasion, a criteria for obtaining a visa or entry into the United States may be waived. This means that the reason for ineligibility will be forgiven or ignored even though a person does not have the proper documents to obtain the visa or enter the United States or is ineligible for entry because of some maleficence such as a criminal act. Almost every reason why an individual will not be allowed to enter the United States can be waived, but waivers are sometimes very difficult to obtain.

BIBLIOGRAPHY

I. Primary Source Materials
(These materials should be available in a large public library or a law school library.)

8 U.S.C.A. §§ 1-1434 — Aliens and Nationality *from*	West Publishing Co. P.O. Box 64833 St. Paul, MN 55164-1804 (800) 328-9352
Code of Federal Regulations (CFR), Title 8 — Aliens and Nationality *from*	Superintendent of Documents U.S. Government Printing Office Washington, D.C. 20402 (202) 783-3238
U.S. Department of State, *Foreign Affairs Manual* (FAM), Vol. 9 — Visas, Operating instructions for Consular Officers *from*	2401 E Street, N.W., Room 800 Washington, D.C. 20520 (202) 647-1105 (Note: FAM consists of 3 parts: general applicability, nonimmi- grants, and immigrants)

II. Other Resources

AILA's *Immigration and* *Nationality Law Handbook* (revised ed. 1992-93) (published annually) *from*	American Immigration Lawyers Association 1400 Eye Street, NW Suite 1200 Washington, DC 20005 (202) 371-9377

Austin T. Fragomen, Alfred J.
Del Rey, Jr., and Steven Bell,
*Immigration Procedures Handbook:
A How to Guide for Legal and
Business Professionals*
(1992 revised ed.)
from

Clark Boardman Company, Ltd.
375 Hudson Street
New York, New York 10014
(800) 221-9428

Charles Gordon & Stanley
Mailman, *Immigration Law and
Procedure* (revised ed. 1986)
(eleven looseleaf volumes,
with 3 months of supplements
and updated periodically)
from

Matthew Bender and Co., Inc.
1275 Broadway
Albany, New York 12201
(800) 833-9844

Charles Gordon & Ellen Gittel
Gordon, *Immigration and
Nationality Law* (supersedes
Immigration and Nationality
Law: Desk Edition) (revised
ed. 1988) (one looseleaf volume, updated with periodic
supplements)
from

Matthew Bender and Co., Inc.
1275 Broadway
Albany, New York 12201
(800) 833-9844

David Weissbrodt, *Immigration
Law and Procedure in a Nutshell*
(1990)
from

West Publishing Co.
P.O. Box 64833
St. Paul, MN 55164-1804
(800) 328-9352

*Employment of F-1 and M-1
Nonimmigrant Students in the
United States* (1990) (describes
the conditions under which
F-1 and M-1 students and their
spouses and children may
lawfully work in the United
States) (6 pages, available in
sets of 100)
from

GPO S/N 027-002-00403-5
Superintendent of Documents
U.S. Government Printing
Office Washington, D.C. 20402
(202) 783-3238

Ira J. Kurzban, *Kurzban's Immigration Law Source Book: A Comprehensive Outline & Reference Tool* (3rd ed. 1992) *from*

American Immigration Law Foundation
1400 Eye Street, N.W., Suite 1200
Washington, D.C. 20005
(202) 371-9377

Interpreter Releases, Maurice Roberts, Editor; Stephen Yale-Loehr, Co-Editor (weekly) *from*

Federal Publications
1120 20th Street, N.W., Suite 500 South
Washington, D.C. 20036
(202) 337-7000

Immigration Briefings, Bruce Hake, Editor (monthly) *from*

Federal Publications
1120 20th Street, N.W., Suite 500 South
Washington, D.C. 20036
(202) 337-7000

"TC" Positions and Requirements for Canadian Professionals

B.A. - bachelors degree; S./P. license - state/provincial

Accountant
B.A.

Architect
B.A. or S./P. license

Computer Systems Analyst
B.A., or post-secondary diploma and three years' experience

Disaster Relief Insurance Claims Adjuster
B.A. or three years' experience in the field of claims adjustment

Economist
B.A.

Engineer
B.A. or S./P. license

Graphic Designer
B.A., or post-secondary diploma and three years' experience

Hotel Manager
B.A. in hotel/restaurant management, or post-secondary diploma in hotel/restaurant management and three years' experience in hotel/restaurant management

Industrial Designer
B.A., or post-secondary diploma and three years' experience

Interior Designer
B.A., or post-secondary diploma and three years' experience

Land Surveyor
B.A. or S./P./F. license

Landscape Architect
B.A.

Lawyer
member of bar in province or state, or L.L.D., J.D., L.L.L., or B.C.L.

Librarian
M.S.S. or B.L.S. (for which another bachelors degree was a prerequisite)

Management Consultant
bachelors degree or five years' experience in consulting or related field

Mathematician
B.A.

MEDICAL ALLIED PROFESSIONALS

Dentist
D.D.S., D.M.D., or S./P. license

Dietician
B.A. or S./P. license

Medical Laboratory
Technologist (Canada)/
Medical Technologist (U.S.) -
*B.A., or post-secondary diploma
and three years' experience*

Nutritional
B.A.

Occupational Therapist
B.A. or S./P. license

Pharmacist
B.A. or S./P. license

Physician (teaching and/or
research only)
M.D. or S./P. license

Physio/physical therapist
B.A. or S./P. license

Psychologist
S./P. license

Recreational therapist
B.A.

Registered Nurse
S./P. license

Veterinarian
D.V.M., D.M.V., or S./P. license

Range Manager
(Range Conservationist)
B.A.

Research Assistant (work-
ing in a post-secondary educational institution)
B.A.

SCIENTIFIC TECHNICIAN/TECHNOLOGICAL

- Must work in direct support of professionals in the following disciplines: agricultural sciences, astronomy,
  biology, chemistry, engineering, forestry, geology, geo-
  physics, meteorology, or physics;

- Must possess theoretical knowledge of the discipline;
  and

- Must solve practical problems in the discipline or
  apply principles of the discipline to basic or applied
  research

SCIENTIST
(all requiring a bachelors degree)

Agriculturist (Agronomist)
Animal Breeder
Animal Scientist
Apiculturist
Astronomer
Biochemist
Biologist
Chemist
Dairy Scientist
Entomologist
Epidemiologist
Geneticist
Geochemist
Geologist
Geophysical
Horticulturist
Meteorologist
Pharmacologist
Physicist
Plant Breeder
Poultry Scientist
Soil Scientist
Social Worker
Syvliculturist
(Forestry Specialist)
Zoologist

TEACHER
(all requiring a bachelors degree)

College
Seminary
University
Technical Publications Writer
*B.A., or post-secondary diploma
and three years' experience*
Urban Planner
Vocational Counselor

ACADEMIC TERMS

As is true of any other people in the world, Americans have developed certain peculiarities in their everyday language. As a student, you are sure to encounter certain colloquialisms and "slang" terms. The following is a list which will give you an idea of the more common of these usages. Also included are terms or vocabulary which you may not have encountered before, but which will prove useful to you during your stay in the United States. No list of this type can even come close to being complete.

Americans like to abbreviate words when they talk. Thus, they are likely to say "ed psych" for educational psychology, "med school" for the College of Medicine, and "bio" for biology. It would be impossible to list all such abbreviations here. If you hear one you do not know, ask someone what it means.

academic adviser - a faculty member appointed to assist a student in planning the student's academic career

add a course - to enter a course in which you were not enrolled at the beginning of the semester

assignment - out-of-class work required by a professor, due by a specified date

blue book - a small booklet of paper with a blue cover, usually used for essay-type examinations

bomb a test - to do poorly on an exam

carrel - a small, enclosed desk in the library reserved by individuals doing research

comps - comprehensive examination, an examination (written, oral, or both) Master's and Ph.D. students take following completion of all the course work required for the degree

cram - to study for a test, usually the night before, in a short period of time - implies that one has not studied the material earlier and must try to condense it into a short period of time

cum - pronounced "kyum" with a long "u", a person's cumulative grade point average

cut - to miss a scheduled class on purpose

cut out - leave

dissertation - a scholarly independent research study required to obtain a doctoral degree

drop a course - to withdraw from a course

drop and add - that period during when students may change their programs of studies by "dropping" and "adding" courses. Also refers to the procedure by which this is done.

final - last exam of a semester

flunk - to fail to achieve a passing grade

fossil - a student who has been on campus a long time

fraternity - a social organization of men, sometimes living together in a large house, each with different rules, regulations, and objectives. Some fraternities are purely social; others are professional organizations or academic honorary organizations

freshman - a student in the first year of study at a college or university (or a four-year secondary school)

G.P.A. - grade point average

graduate or grad student - a student who has earned a bachelors and is pursuing a higher degree

Greek - member of a fraternity or a sorority

honor system - the practice of relying on students not to cheat in any academic matter

incomplete - a temporary mark at some colleges given to a student who is doing passing work in a course but who cannot complete all the requirements for the course during the term. Indicated by an "I" on a student's grade report.

jock course - a course in which it is generally considered to be easy to receive a good grade with a minimum of work

junior - a student in the third year of study at a college or university

major - a student's primary field of study

matriculate - to formally enroll in a college or university; to register for classes

McPaper - a paper that is done in a hurry without much research

minor - a student's secondary field of study

mid-term - test in the middle of a semester

orals - the oral examinations which a student working toward a doctor's degree must pass in order to become a "candidate" for a Ph.D. degree. It is a preliminary test of the student's knowledge in the field

prof - a professor

quiz - a short test, usually given without warning reading list (syllabus) - a list of books and articles prepared by each professor for a specific course. Required and suggested texts are usually indicated as such. This list is designed to give the student an overview of the particular course

registrar - official recorder of students' academic information, such as courses taken and grades received

registration - procedure of enrolling officially in classes at the beginning of each semester

semester - one academic term, which is half of the academic year. Some colleges and universities are on the quarter system with three quarters of study equaling one academic year.

senior - a student in the forth year of study at a college or university

skim - to quickly read something to get a general idea of its contents

skipped, skip out - to fail to attend a class or meeting

sophomore - a student in the second year of study at a college or university

sorority - comparable to a fraternity, except that it is for females instead of males

T.A. - teaching assistant

thesis - a scholarly research paper which may be required to obtain a master's degree

transcript - official record of a student's grades and courses

undergraduate - a student in the first four (4) years of university study

LIST OF NONIMMIGRANT VISAS

A-1   Ambassador, public minister, career diplomat, or consular office, and immediate family

A-2   Other foreign government official or employee, and immediate family

A-3   Attendant, servant, or personal employee of A-1 or A-2, and immediate family

B-1   Temporary visitor for business

B-2   Temporary visitor for pleasure

C-1   Alien in transit

C-2   Alien in transit to United Nations Headquarters district under Section 11(3), (4), or (5) of the Headquarters Agreement

C-3   Foreign government official, immediate family, attendant, servant, or personal employee, in transit

D   Crewmember (sea or air)

E-1   Treaty trader, spouse, and children

E-2   Treaty investor, spouse, and children

F-1   Student

F-2   Spouse or child of student

G-1   Principal resident representative of recognized foreign member government of international organization, staff, and immediate family

G-2   Other representative or recognized foreign member government to international organization, and immediate family

G-3   Representative of nonrecognized or nonmember foreign government of international organization, and immediate family

G-4   International organization officer or employee, and immediate family

H-1A   Registered Nurse

H-1B   Alien in a specialty occupation (professional)

H-2A   Temporary worker performing agricultural services unavailable in the United States

H-2B   Temporary worker performing other services unavailable in the United States

H-3   Trainee

H-4   Spouse or child of alien classified in one of these H categories

I   Representative of foreign media, spouse, and children

J-1   Exchange visitor

J-2   Spouse of child of exchange visitor

K-1   Fiance(e) of U.S. citizen

K-2   Child of fiance(e) of U.S. citizen

L-1   Intracompany transferee (executive, managerial, and specialized personnel continuing employment with international firm or corporation)

L-2   Spouse or child of intercompany transferee

M-1   Vocational student or other nonacademic student

M-2   Spouse or child of vocational student

N-8   Parent of an alien classified SK-3 special immigrant

N-9   Child of N-8 or of an SK-1, SK-2, or SK-4 special immigrant

NATO   Representatives, staff, family members, dependents, and personal employees of the preceding affiliated with NATO

O-1   Aliens with extraordinary ability in sciences, arts, education, business, or athletics

0-2   Accompanying alien to an O-1 principal

0-3   Spouse/child of O-1 principal or O-2 accompanying alien

P-1   Internationally recognized athlete or member of internationally recognized entertainment group

P-2   Artist or entertainer in a reciprocal exchange program

P-3   Artist or entertainer in a culturally unique program

Q-1   Participant in an international cultural exchange program

R-1   Alien in a religious occupation

R-2   Spouse or child of an alien in a religious occupation

HOW TO FIND AN IMMIGRATION LAWYER

While this Handbook tries to guide you though the basics of immigration law as it affects students, no book or advice can replace the assistance of an experienced immigration lawyer. Immigration lawyers are fully authorized to counsel and represent students before the Immigration and Naturalization Service, are completely accountable to their licensing authority, and oftentimes are surprisingly affordable. When you find you need advice, there are resources available to help you find a good attorney.

ASK YOUR FOREIGN STUDENT ADVISOR FOR REFERRALS

Your foreign student advisor can be very helpful in referring you to a seasoned immigration attorney. He or she may be familiar with the reputation and expertise of a number of lawyers.

TALK TO FRIENDS

Sometimes, friends who have been in your situation have turned to immigration lawyers for advice. Ask them if they have an attorney they can recommend.

CONTACT YOUR LOCAL BAR ASSOCIATION

Virtually every large city in the United States has one or more associations of attorneys, called "bar associations".

Oftentimes, they have referral services to attorneys in that area, and can refer you to an attorney with expertise in immigration law.

CONTACT THE AMERICAN IMMIGRATION LAWYERS ASSOCIATION

You could also seek a referral from the National Office of the American Immigration Lawyers Association, known also as AILA. AILA is a professional association made up of thousands of immigration lawyers, that provides its members with opportunities for advanced legal education and up-to-date immigration information. You could contact the address below for the Chapter of immigration lawyers nearest you, who will then be able to refer you to a particular lawyer in your community. That address is: American Immigration Lawyers Association, 1400 Eye Street, NW, Suite 1200, Washington, DC 20005, telephone (202) 371-9377.

CONTACT ACCREDITED REPRESENTATIVES IN YOUR AREA

If you are low-income and cannot locate an attorney to assist you, you may want to talk with a not-for-profit immigration assistance service with "accredited representatives". Accredited representatives are authorized by the Immigration and Naturalization Service to assist persons with immigration problems, and if employed by a not-for-profit organization, may be able to provide legal services for free or at a low fee. Your foreign student advisor may be able to direct you to some.

*Don't be afraid to shop around
for the best advice.*

INS DISTRICT OFFICES

Albany Suboffice
James T. Foley
Federal Courthouse
445 Broadway, Rm. 227
Albany, NY 12207
(518) 472-7140
General: (518) 472-2434

Albuqerque Suboffice
517 Gold Southwest Ave.
Rm. 1114
Albuqerque, NM 87103
(506) 766-2378

Anchorage District
INS
Suite 102
620 East 10th Ave.
Anchorage, AK 99501-7581
(907) 271-3101

Atlanta District
77 Forsyth Street S.W.
Room G-85
Atlanta, GA 30303
(404) 331-0253

Baltimore District
E.A. Garmatz Federal Bldg.
101 West Lombard Street
Baltimore, MD 21202
(301) 962-2120/2010

Boston District
John Fitzgerald Kennedy
 Federal Bldg.
Rm. 700, Gov't Center
Boston, MA 02203
(617) 565-4943

Buffalo District
U.S. Courthouse
68 Court S., Rm. 113
Buffalo, NY 14202
(716) 849-4741

Charleston Suboffice
Federal Bldg., Rm. 330
334 Meeting St.
Charleston, SC 29402
(803) 727-4422/4359

Charlotte Suboffice
6 Woodlawn Green, Ste. 138
Charlotte, NC 28217
(704) 523-1704

Chicago District
10 West Jackson Blvd.
Chicago, IL 60604
(312) 353-7302

Cincinnati Suboffice
J.W. Peck Federal Bldg.
550 Main Street, Rm. 8525
P.O. Box 537
Cincinnati, OH 45202
(513) 684-2930

Cleveland District
Anthony J. Celebreeze
Federal Office Bldg.
Rm. 1917
1240 East 9th Street
Cleveland, OH 44199
(216) 522-4767

Dallas District
3101 N. Stemmons Fwy.
Dallas, TX 75247
(214) 655-3011

Denver District
Albrook Center
4730 Paris Street
Denver, CO 80239
(303) 371-3041/0986

Detroit District
Federal Building, INS
333 Mt. Elliot Street
(313) 226-3250

El Paso District
700 East San Antonio
El Paso, TX 79984
(915) 543-6366/6334

Fresno Suboffice
U.S. Courthouse, Federal Bldg.
Rm 1308, 1130 ISt.
Fresno, CA 93721
(209) 487-5091/5646

Guam Suboffice
801 Pacific News Bldg.
238 O'Hara Street
Agana, Guam 96910
(671) 472-6411

Harlingen District
2102 Teege Road
Harlingen, TX 78550
(512) 425-7342

Hartford Suboffice
3060 Ribicoff Fed. Bldg.
450 Main St.
Hartford, CT 06130-3060
(203) 240-3050

Helena District
Federal Building, Rm. 512
301 South Park, Drawer 10036
Helena, MT 59626-0036
(406) 449-5288

Honolulu District
595 Ala Moana Bouelvard
P.O. Box 461
Honolulu, HI 96813
(808) 541-1388

Houston District
509 North Belt
Houston, TX 77060
(713) 229-2908

Indianapolis Suboffice
46 East Ohio Street, Rm. 124
Indianapolis, IN 46204
(317) 226-6009

Jacksonville Suboffice
Federal Building
400 W. Bay St., Rm. G-28
Jacksonville, FL 32202
(904) 791-2624/3156

Kansas City District
9747 N. Conant Ave.
Kansas City, MO 64153
(816) 891-9318

Las Vegas Suboffice
Fed. Bldg., Rm. 104
U.S. Courthouse
300 Las Vegas Blvd. SO
Las Vegas, NV 89101

Louisville Suboffice
U.S. Courthouse Bldg.
West 6th & Broadway
Rm. 601
Louisville, KY 40202
(502) 582-6375

Los Angeles District
300 N. Los Angeles St.
Room 1000
Los Angeles, CA 90012
(213) 894-2780/2782

Memphis Suboffice
Federal Bldg., Rm. 830
167 N. Main St.
Memphis, TN 38103
(901)544-4056

Miami District
7880 Biscayne Blvd.
Miami, FL 33138
(305) 530-7657

Milwaukee Suboffice
Federal Bldg., Rm. 186
517 East Wisconsin Ave.
Milwaukee, WI 53202
(414) 291-3565

Newark District
Federal Bldg.
970 Broad Street
Newark, NJ 07102
(201) 645-2269

New Orleans District
Postal Service Bldg.
Rm. T-8005
701 Loyola Avenue
New Orleans, LA 70113
(504) 589-6533

New York District
26 Federal Plaza, Rm. 14-102
New York, NY 10278
(212) 264-5942

Norfolk Suboffice
Norfolk Federal Bldg.
200 Granby Mall, Rm. 439
Norfolk, VA 23510
(804) 441-3081

Oklahoma City Suboffice
4149 Highline Blvd.
Suite 300
Oklahoma City, OK 73108
(405) 942-8670

Omaha District
3736 S. 32nd St.
Omaha, NE 68144
(402) 697-9152

Philadelphia District
U.S. Courthouse
Independence Mall W.
1600 Callowhill St.
Philadelphia, PA 19130
(215) 656-7150

Phoenix District
Federal Building
230 N. First Ave.
Phoenix, AZ 85025
(602) 379-6666

Pittsburgh Suboffice
2130 Federal Bldg.
1000 Liberty Ave.
Pittsburgh. PA 15222
(412) 644-3356

Portland, ME District
739 Warren Ave.
Portland, ME 04103
(207) 780-3352

Portland, OR District
Federal Office Bldg.
511 N.W. Broadway
Portland, OR 97209
(505) 221-2155
(503) 221-2271 (General)

Providence Suboffice
203 John O. Pastore Fed. Bldg.
Providence, RI 02903
(401) 528-5323
General: (401) 454-7440

Reno Suboffice
712 Mill Street
Reno, NV 89502
(702) 784-5644

Riviera Beach Suboffice
4 East Port Road, Rm 129
P.O. Box 9846
Riviera Beach, FL 33404
(305) 844-4341

Sacramento Suboffice
711 "J" St.
Sacramento, CA 95814
(916) 551-3116

St. Albans Suboffice
Federal Bldg., P.O. Box 328
St. Albans, VT 05478
(802) 524-6742

St. Croix District
P.O. Box 1270, Kinghill
Christian Sted, St. Croix
Virgin Islands 00850
(809) 773-7559

St. Louis Suboffice
1222 Spruce St., Suite 1100
St. Louis, MO 63103
(314) 539-2532

St. Paul District
2901 Metro Dr., Ste. 100
Bloomington, MN 55425
(612) 335-2211

St. Thomas Suboffice
Federal District Court Bldg.
P.O. Box 610
Charlotte Amalie
St. Thomas, VI 00801
(809) 774-1390

Salt Lake City Suboffice
230 W. 400 South St.
Salt Lake City, UT 84101
(801) 524-6272

San Antonio District
U.S. Federal Bldg., Ste. A301
727 E. Durango
San Antonio, TX 78206
(512) 871-7000

San Diego District
880 Frong St., Rm. 1-S-13
San Diego, CA 92188
(619) 557-5570/5645

San Francisco District
Appraisers Building
630 Sansome St.
San Francisco, CA 94111
(415) 556-4411/4571

San Jose Suboffice
280 S. First St.
San Jose, CA 95113
(408) 291-7027
(408) 291-4256
(408) 291-7876 (General)

San Juan District
Fed. Bldg., Rm. 380
Chardon St.
Hato Ray, PR 00936
or

P.O. Box 365063
San Juan, PR 00936
(809) 766-7479/5380

Seattle District
815 Airport Way South
Seattle, WA 98134
(206) 553-5956/0070

Spokane Suboffice
691 U.S. Courthouse Bldg.
West 920 Riverside
Spokane, WA 99201
(509) 624-1109

Tampa Suboffice
5509 West Gray Street
Suite 114
Tampla, FL 33609-1059
(813) 228-2131

Tucson Suboffice
Federal Building
Rm. 1-T, FB-37
301 W. Congress
Tucson, AZ 85701
(602) 629-6229

Washington, DC District
4420 N. Fairfax Dr.
Arlington, VA 22203
(202) 307-1501/1640

Westminster Suboffice
14560 Magnolia St.
Westminster, CA
No Phone Given

LIST OF FORMS

Following are the immigration-related forms that foreign students are most likely to see:

ETA-9035   Labor Condition Application (LCA) for H-1B Nonimmigrants

G-325A   Biographic Information

I-20A-B   Certificate of Eligibility for Nonimmigrant (F-1) Student Status — For Academic and Language Students

I-20M-N   Certificate of Eligibility for Nonimmigrant (M-1) Student Status — For Vocational Students

I-94   Arrival/Departure Record

I-134   Affidavit of Support

I-538	Application by Nonimmigrant Student for Extension of Stay, School Transfer, or Permission to Accept or Continue Employment
I-539	Application to Extend/Change of Nonimmigrant Status
I-765	Application for Employment Authorization
IAP-66	Certificate of Eligibility for Exchange Visitor (J-1) Status
OF-156	Nonimmigrant Visa Application

SAMPLE FORMS

The following pages illustrate some of the forms discussed in the text.

U.S. Department of Justice
Immigration and Naturalization Service
Please Read Instructions on Page 2

Certificate of Eligibility for Nonimmigrant (F-1) Student
Status - For Academic and Language Students

OMB No. 1115-0051

Page 1

This page must be completed and signed in the U.S. by a designated school official.

For Immigration Official Use

Visa issuing post	Date Visa issued

Reinstated, extension granted to:

1. Family Name (surname)

First (given) name (do not enter middle name)

Country of birth	Date of birth (mo./day/year)

Country of citizenship	Admission number (Complete if known)

2. School (school district) name

School official to be notified of student's arrival in U.S. (Name and Title)

School address (include zip code)

School code (including 3-digit suffix, if any) and approval date

214F _____ approved on _____

3. This certificate is issued to the student named above for:
(Check and fill out as appropriate)

a. ☐ Initial attendance at this school.
b. ☐ Continued attendance at this school.
c. ☐ School transfer.
   Transferred from _____.
d. ☐ Use by dependents for entering the United States.
e. ☐ Other _____

7. This school estimates the student's average costs for an academic term of
_____ (up to 12) months to be:

a. Tuition and fees $ _____
b. Living expenses $ _____
c. Expenses of dependents $ _____
d. Other (specify): $ _____

Total $ _____

I-20 SCHOOL

4. Level of education the student is pursuing or will pursue in the United States: (check only one)

a. ☐ Primary   e. ☐ Master's

b. ☐ Secondary   f. ☐ Doctorate

c. ☐ Associate   g. ☐ Language training

d. ☐ Bachelor's   h. ☐ Other

5. The student named above has been accepted for a full course of study at

this school, majoring in _____.

The student is expected to report to the school not later than (date) _____

and complete studies not later than (date) _____.

The normal length of study is _____.

6. ☐ English proficiency is required:

    ☐ The student has the required English proficiency.

    ☐ The student is not yet proficient, English instructions will be given at the school.

    ☐ English proficiency is not required because _____

8. This school has information showing the following as the student's means of support, estimated for an academic term of _____ months (Use the same number of months given in Item 7).

a. Student's personal funds $ _____

b. Funds from this school (specify type) $ _____

c. Funds from another source (specify type and source) $ _____

d. On-campus employment (if any) $ _____

        Total $ _____

9. Remarks: _____

10. School Certification: I certify under penalty of perjury that all information provided above in items 1 through 8 was completed before I signed this form and is true and correct; I executed this form in the United States after review and evaluation in the United States by me or other officials of the school of the student's application, transcripts or other records of courses taken and proof of financial responsibility, which were received at the school prior to the execution of this form; the school has determined that the above named student's qualifications meet all standards for admission to the school; the student will be required to pursue a full course of study as defined by 8 CFR 214.2(f)(6); I am a designated official of the above named school and I am authorized to issue this form.

_____   _____   _____   _____   _____

Signature of designated school official   Name of school official (print or type)   Title   Date issued   Place issued (city and state)

11. Student Certification: I have read and agreed to comply with the terms and conditions of my admission and those of any extension of stay as specified on page 2. I certify that all information provided on this form refers specifically to me and is true and correct to the best of my knowledge. I certify that I seek to enter or remain in the United States temporarily, and solely for the purpose of pursuing a full course of study at the school named on Page 1 of this form. I also authorize the named school to release any information from my records which is needed by the INS pursuant to 8 CFR 214.3(g) to determine my nonimmigrant status.

_____   _____   _____

Signature of student   Name of student   Date

Authority for collecting the information on this and related student forms is contained in 8 U.S.C. 1101 and 1184. The information solicited will be used by the Department of State and the Immigration and Naturalization Service to determine eligibility for the benefits requested.

INSTRUCTIONS TO DESIGNATED SCHOOL OFFICIALS

1. The law provides severe penalties for knowingly and willfully falsifying or concealing a material fact, or using any false document in the submission of this form. Designated school officials should consult regulations pertaining to the issuance of Form I-20 A-B at 8 CFR 214.3 (K) before completing this form. Failure to comply with these regulations may result in the withdrawal of the school approval for attendance by foreign students by the Immigration and Naturalization Service (8 CFR 214.4).

2. ISSUANCE OF FORM I-20 A-B. Designated school officials may issue a Form I-20 A-B to a student who fits into one of the following categories, if the student has been accepted for full-time attendance at the institution: a) a prospective F-1 nonimmigrant student; b) an F-1 transfer student; c) an F-1 student advancing to a higher educational level at the same institution; d) an out of status student seeking reinstatement. The form may also be issued to the dependent spouse or child of an F-1 student for securing entry into the United States.

When issuing a Form I-20 A-B, designated school officials should complete the student's admission number whenever possible to ensure proper data entry and record keeping.

3. ENDORSEMENT OF PAGE 4 FOR REENTRY. Designated school officials may endorse page 4 of the Form I-20 A-B for reentry if the student and/or the F-2 dependents is to leave the United States temporarily. This should be done only when the information on the Form I-20 remains unchanged. If there have been substantial changes in item 4, 5, 7, or 8, a new Form I-20 A-B should be issued.

4 REPORTING REQUIREMENT. Designated school official should always forward the top page of the Form I-20 A-B to the INS data proces-

---

dent in an educational program and any period of authorized practical training plus sixty days. While in the United States, you must maintain a valid foreign passport unless you are exempt from passport requirements.

You may continue from one educational level to another, such as progressing from high school to a bachelor's program or a bachelor's program to a master's program, etc., simply by invoking the procedures for school transfers.

3. SCHOOL. For initial admission, you must attend the school specified on your visa. If you have a Form I-20 A-B from more than one school, it is important to have the name of the school you intend to attend specified on your visa by presenting a Form I-20 A-B from that school to the visa issuing consular officer. Failure to attend the specified school will result in the loss of your student status and subject you to deportation.

4. REENTRY. A nonimmigrant student may be readmitted after a temporary absence of five months or less from the United States, if the student is otherwise admissible. You may be readmitted by presenting a valid foreign passport, a valid visa, and either a new Form I-20 A-B or a page 4 of the Form I-20 A-B (the I-20 ID Copy) properly endorsed for reentry if the information on the I-20 form is current.

5. TRANSFER. A nonimmigrant student is permitted to transfer to a different school provided the transfer procedure is followed. To transfer school, you should first notify the school you are attending of the intent to transfer, then obtain a Form I-20 A-B from the school you intend to attend. Transfer will be effected only if you return the Form I-20 A-B to the designated school official within 15 days of beginning attendance at the new school. The designated school official will then report the transfer to the Immigration and Naturalization Service.

6. EXTENSION OF STAY. If you cannot complete the educational program after having been in student status for longer than the anticipated length of the program plus a grace period in a single educational level, or for more than eight consecutive years, you must apply for extension of stay. An application for extension of stay on a Form I-538 should be filed with the Immigration and Naturalization Service district office having jurisdiction over your school at least 15 days but no more than 60 days before the expiration of your authorized stay.

7. **EMPLOYMENT.** As an F-1 student, you are not permitted to work off-campus or to engage in business without specific employment authorization. After your first year in F-1 student status, you may apply for employment authorization on Form I-538 based on financial needs arising after receiving student status, or the need to obtain practical training.

8. **Notice of Address.** If you move, you must submit a notice within 10 days of the change of address to the Immigration and Naturalization Service. (Form AR-11 is available at any INS office.)

9. **Arrival/Departure.** When you leave the United States, you must surrender your Form I-94 Departure Record. Please see the back side of Form I-94 for detailed instructions. You do not have to turn in the I-94 if you are visiting Canada, Mexico, or adjacent islands other than Cuba for less than 30 days.

10. **Financial Support.** You must demonstrate that you are financially able to support yourself for the entire period of stay in the United States while pursuing a full course of study. You are required to attach documentary evidence of means of support.

11. **Authorization to Release Information by School.** To comply with requests from the United States Immigration & Naturalization Service for information concerning your immigration status, you are required to give authorization to the named school to release such information from your records. The school will provide the Service your name, country of birth, current address, and any other information on a regular basis or upon request.

12. **Penalty.** To maintain your nonimmigrant student status, you must be enrolled as a full-time student at the school you are authorized to attend. You may engage in employment only when you have received permission to work. Failure to comply with these regulations will result in the loss of your student status and subject you to deportation.

sing center at P.O. Box 140, London, Kentucky 40741 for data entry except when the form is issued to an F-1 student for initial entry or reentry into the United States, or for reinstatement to student status. (Requests for reinstatement should be sent to the Immigration and Naturalization Service district office having jurisdiction over the student's temporary residence in this country.)

The INS data processing center will return this top page to the issuing school for disposal after data entry and microfilming.

5. **CERTIFICATION.** Designated school officials should certify on the bottom part of page 1 of this form that the Form I-20 A-B is completed and issued in accordance with the pertinent regulations. The designated school official should remove the carbon sheet from the completed and signed Form I-20 A-B before forwarding it to the student.

6. **ADMISSION RECORDS.** Since the Immigration and Naturalization Service may request information concerning the student's immigration status for various reasons, designated school officials should retain all evidence which shows the scholastic ability and financial status on which admission was based, until the school has reported the student's termination of studies to the Immigration and Naturalization Service.

INSTRUCTIONS TO STUDENTS

1. **Student Certification.** You should read everything on this page carefully and be sure that you understand the terms and conditions concerning your admission and stay in the United States as a nonimmigrant student before you sign the student certification on the bottom part of page 1. **The law provides severe penalties for knowingly and willfully falsifying or concealing a material fact, or using any false document in the submission of this form.**

2. **ADMISSION.** A nonimmigrant student may be admitted for duration of status. This means that you are authorized to stay in the United States for the entire length of time during which you are enrolled as a full-time stu-

Page 3

Immigration and Naturalization Service Status - For Academic and Language Students

Please Read Instructions on Page 2

This page must be completed and signed in the U.S. by a designated school official.

1. Family Name (surname)

   First (given) name (do not enter middle name)

   Date of birth (mo./day/year)

   Country of birth

   Country of citizenship   Admission number (Complete if known)

2. School (school district) name

   School official to be notified of student's arrival in U.S. (Name and Title)

   School address (include zip code)

   School code (including 3-digit suffix, if any) and approval date
   214F _____ approved on _____

3. This certificate is issued to the student named above for:
   (Check and fill out as appropriate)

   a. ☐ Initial attendance at this school.

   b. ☐ Continued attendance at this school.

   c. ☐ School transfer.
      Transferred from _____.

   d. ☐ Use by dependents for entering the United States.

   e. ☐ Other _____.

For Immigration Official Use

Visa issuing post   Date Visa issued

Reinstated, extension granted to:

7. This school estimates the student's average costs for an academic term of _____ (up to 12) months to be:

   a. Tuition and fees $ _____
   b. Living expenses $ _____
   c. Expenses of dependents $ _____
   d. Other (specify): _____ $ _____

   Total $ _____

I-20-ID (STUDENT) COPY

4. Level of education the student is pursuing or will pursue in the United States:

(check only one)

a. ☐ Primary   e. ☐ Master's

b. ☐ Secondary   f. ☐ Doctorate

c. ☐ Associate   g. ☐ Language training

d. ☐ Bachelor's   h. ☐ Other

5. The student named above has been accepted for a full course of study at

this school, majoring in _____.

The student is expected to report to the school not later than (date) _____

and complete studies not later than (date) _____.

The normal length of study is _____.

6. ☐ English proficiency is required:

   ☐ The student has the required English proficiency.

   ☐ The student is not yet proficient, English instructions will be given at

     the school.

   ☐ English proficiency is not required because _____

8. This school has information showing the following as the student's means of

support, estimated for an academic term of _____ months (Use the same

number of months given in item 7).

a. Student's personal funds $ _____

b. Funds from this school $ _____

(specify type)

c. Funds from another source $ _____

(specify type and source)

d. On-campus employment (if any) $ _____

Total $ _____

9. Remarks: _____

10. **School Certification:** I certify under penalty of perjury that all information provided above in items 1 through 8 was completed before I signed this form and is true and correct; I executed this form in the United States after review and evaluation in the United States by me or other officials of the school of the student's application, transcripts or other records of courses taken and proof of financial responsibility, which were received at the school prior to the execution of this form; the school has determined that the above named student's qualifications meet all standards for admission to the school; the student will be required to pursue a full course of study as defined by 8 CFR 214.2(f)(6); I am a designated official of the above named school and I am authorized to issue this form.

_____ _____ _____ _____ _____

Signature of designated school official   Name of school official (print or type)   Title   Date issued   Place issued (city and state)

11. **Student Certification:** I have read and agreed to comply with the terms and conditions of my admission and those of any extension of stay as specified on page 2. I certify that all information provided on this form refers specifically to me and is true and correct to the best of my knowledge. I certify that I seek to enter or remain in the United States temporarily, and solely for the purpose of pursuing a full course of study at the school named on Page 1 of this form. I also authorize the named school to release any information from my records which is needed by the INS pursuant to 8 CFR 214.3(g) to determine my nonimmigrant status.

_____ _____ _____

Signature of student   Name of student   Date

_____ _____ _____ _____ _____

Signature of parent or guardian   Name of parent/guardian (Print or type)   Address(city)   (State or province)   (Country)   (Date)

if student is under 18

THIS PAGE, WHEN PROPERLY ENDORSED, MAY BE USED FOR ENTRY OF THE SPOUSE AND CHILDREN OF AN F-1 STUDENT FOLLOWING TO JOIN THE STUDENT IN THE UNITED STATES OR FOR REENTRY OF THE STUDENT TO ATTEND THE SAME SCHOOL AFTER A TEMPORARY ABSENCE FROM THE UNITED STATES.

For reentry of the student and/or the F-2 dependents (EACH CERTIFICATION SIGNATURE IS VALID FOR ONLY ONE YEAR.)

Signature of Designated School Official	Name of School Official (print or type)	Title	Date
Signature of Designated School Official	Name of School Official (print or type)	Title	Date
Signature of Designated School Official	Name of School Official (print or type)	Title	Date
Signature of Designated School Official	Name of School Official (print or type)	Title	Date
Signature of Designated School Official	Name of School Official (print or type)	Title	Date
Signature of Designated School Official	Name of School Official (print or type)	Title	Date

Dependent spouse and children of the F-1 student who are seeking entry/reentry to the U.S.

Name family (caps) first	Date of birth	Country of birth	Relationship to the F-1 student

Student Employment Authorization and other Records

U.S. Department of Justice
Immigration and Naturalization Service

OMB Approval No. 1115-0060
Certification by Designated School Official

SECTION A. This section must be completed by student as appropriate (Please print or type) :

1. Name: (Family in CAPS)   (First)   (Middle)   2. Date of birth:

3. Student admission number:

4. Date first granted F-1 or M-1 status:

5. Level of education being sought:

6. Student's major field of study:

7. Describe the proposed employment for practical training:

Beginning date :   Ending date: Number of hours per week:

8. List all periods of previously authorized employment for practical training:

A. Curricular or work/study:	B. Post completion of studies		

Signature of student: _____ Date: _____

SECTION B. This Section must be completed by the designated school official of the school the student is attending or was last authorized to attend:

9. I hereby certify that:

The student named above:

☐ Is taking a full course of study at this school, and the expected date of completion is: _____

☐ Is taking less than a full course of study at this school because: _____

☐ Completed the course of study at this school on (date): _____

☐ Did not complete the course of study. Terminated attendance on (date): _____

Check one:

☐ A. The employment is for practical training in the student's field of study. The student has been in the educational program for at least 9 months and is eligible for the requested practical training in accordance with INS regulations at 8CFR 214.2(f) (10).

☐ B. The endorsement for off-campus employment is based on the wage-and-labor attestation filed by the employer in accordance with the requirements set forth by the Secretary of Labor. The student has been in F-1 status for at least one year and is in good academic standing. Copy of the employer's attestation is attached.

☐ C. The employment is for an internship with a recognized international organization and is within the scope of the organization's sponsorship. The student has been in F-1 status for at least 9 months and is in good academic standing.

10. Name and title of DSO:	Signature:	Date:
11. Name of school:	School file number:	Telephone no.:

For Official Use only

Microfilm Index Number:

Form I-538 (Rev. 10/29/91)N

(See instructions on reverse)

Instructions

A Student seeking authorization for off-campus employment (F-1 only) or practical training (F-1 and M-1) must submit as supporting documentation to Form I-765, Application for Employment Authorization, a certification by the designated school official (DSO) of the school they were last authorized to attend. Certification by the DSO is required of all students (F-1 and M-1) seeking authorization for employment off campus or practical training, including required or optional curricular practical training. The DSO must certify on Form I-538 that the proposed employment is directly related to the student's field of study. A copy of the DSO's certification must be mailed to the STSC date processing center, P.O. Box 140, Highway 25 South, London, Ky. 40741.

All students requesting school certification must complete questions 1 through 6. Students requesting recommendation for practical training must complete questions 7 and 8. Answers to questions 7 through 9 may be continued on this page if needed.

M-1 students seeking extensions of stay must submit a completed Form I-539, Application to Extend time of Temporary Stay, supported by a current Form I-20M-N as appropriate.

Reporting Burden

Public reporting burden for this collection of information is estimated to average 4 minutes per response, including the time for reviewing instructions, searching existing data sources, gathering and maintaining the data needed, and completing and reviewing the collection of information. Send comments regarding this burden estimate or any other aspect of this collection of information, including suggestions for reducing this burden, to: U.S. Department of Justice, Immigration and Naturalization Service (Room 5304), Washington, D.C. 20536; and to the Office Management and Budget, Paperwork Reduction Project, OMB No. 1115-0060 Washington, D.C. 20503.

Comments:

Form I-538 (10/29/91)N

U. S. Department of Justice
Immigration and Naturalization Service

Application for Employment Authorization

How to File:

A separate application must be filed by each applicant. Applications must be typewritten or clearly printed in ink and completed in full. If extra space is needed to answer any item, attach a continuation sheet and indicate your name, A-number (if any) and the item number.

Note: It is recommended that you retain a complete copy of your application for your records.

Who should file this application?

Certain aliens temporarily in the United States are eligible for employment authorization. Please refer to the ELIGIBILITY SECTION of this application which is found on page three. Carefully review the classes of aliens described in Group A and Group C to determine if you are eligible to apply.

This application should not be filed by lawful permanent resident aliens or by lawful temporary resident aliens.

What is the fee?

Applicants must pay a fee of $35.00 to file this form unless otherwise noted on the reverse of the form.

What is our authority for collecting this information?

The authority to require you to file Form I-765, Application for Employment Authorization, is contained in the "Immigration Reform and Control Act of 1986." This information is necessary to determine whether you are eligible for employment authorization and for the preparation of your Employment Authorization Document if you are found eligible. Failure to provide all information as requested may result in the denial or rejection of this application.

The information you provide may also be disclosed to other federal, state, local and foreign law enforcement and regulatory agencies during the course of the investigation required by this Service.

Basic Criteria to Establish Economic Necessity:

Title 45 - Public Welfare, Poverty Guidelines, 45 CFR 1060.2 may be used as the basic criteria to establish eligibility for employment authorization when the applicant's economic necessity is identified as a factor. If you are an applicant who must show economic necessity, you should include a statement listing all of your assets, income, and expenses as evidence of your economic need to work.

Please refer to page 3. If required, the fee will not be refunded. Pay by cash, check, or money order in the exact amount. All checks and money orders must be payable in U.S. currency in the United States. Make check or money order payable to "Immigration and Naturalization Service." However, if you live in Guam make it payable to "Treasurer, Guam," or if you live in the U.S. Virgin Islands make it payable to "Commissioner of Finance of the Virgin Islands." If the check is not honored the INS will charge you $5.00.

Where should you file this application?

Applications must be filed with the nearest Immigration and Naturalization Service (INS) office that processes employment authorization applications which has jurisdiction over your place of residence. You must appear in person to receive an employment authorization document. **Please bring your INS Form I-94 and any document issued to you by the INS granting you previous employment authorization.**

Note: Not all applicants are required to establish economic necessity. Carefully review the ELIGIBILITY SECTION of the application. Only aliens who are filing for employment authorization under Group C, items (c)(3) (i), (c)(13), (c)(14) and (c) (18) are required to furnish information on economic need. This information must be furnished on attached sheet(s) and submitted with this application.

What are the penalties for submitting false information?

Title 18, United States Code, Section 1001 states that whoever **willfully** and knowingly falsifies a material fact, makes a false statement, or makes use of a false document will be fined up to $10,000 or imprisoned up to five years, or both.

Title 18, United States Code, Section 1546(a) states that whoever makes any false statement with respect to a material fact in any document required by the immigration laws or regulations, or presents an application containing any false statement shall be fined or imprisoned or both.

Please Complete Both Sides of Form.

Reporting Burden: Public reporting burden for this collection of information is estimated to average sixty (60) minutes per response, including the time for reviewing instructions, searching existing data sources, gathering and maintaining the data needed, and completing and reviewing the collection of information. Send comments regarding this burden estimate or any other aspect of this collection of information, including suggestions for reducing this burden, to: U.S. Department of Justice, Immigration and Naturalization Service, Room 2011, Washington, D.C. 20536; and to the Office of Management and Budget, Paperwork Reduction Project: OMB No. 1115-0163, Washington, D.C. 20503.

U. S. Department of Justice
Immigration and Naturalization Service

OMB # 1115-0163
Application for Employment Authorization

Please Complete Both Sides of Form

Do Not Write In This Block

Remarks	Action Stamp	Fee Stamp

A#

Applicant is filing under 274a.12

☐ Application Approved. Employment Authorized / Extended (Circle One) _____ (Date).
until _____ (Date).

Subject to the following conditions: _____

☐ Application Denied.
  ☐ Failed to establish eligibility under 8 CFR 274a.12 (a) or (c).
  ☐ Failed to establish economic necessity as required in 8 CFR 274a.12(c) (13) (14) (18) and 8 CFR 214.2(f)

I am applying for: ☐ Permission to accept employment
                    ☐ Replacement (of lost employment authorization document).
                    ☐ Extension of my permission to accept employment (attach previous employment authorization document).

1. Name (Family Name in CAPS)   (First)   (Middle)

2. Other Names Used (Include Maiden Name)

3. Address in the United States (Number and Street)   (Apt. Number)

   (Town or City)   (State/Country)   (ZIP Code)

4. Country of Citizenship/Nationality

5. Place of Birth (Town or City) (State/Province)   (Country)

11. Have you ever before applied for employment authorization from INS?
    ☐ Yes (If yes, complete below)   ☐ No
    Which INS Office?   Date(s)

    Results (Granted or Denied - attach all documentation)

12. Date of Last Entry into the U.S. (Month/Day/Year)

13. Place of Last Entry into the U.S.

14. Manner of Last Entry (Visitor, Student, etc.)

6. Date of Birth (Month/Day/Year)

7. Sex
☐ Male ☐ Female

8. Marital Status ☐ Married ☐ Single
☐ Widowed ☐ Divorced

9. Social Security Number (Include all Numbers you have ever used)

10. Alien Registration Number (A-Number) or I-94 Number (if any)

15. Current Immigration Status (Visitor, Student, etc.)

16. Go to the Eligibility Section on the reverse of this form and check the box which applies to you. In the space below, place the letter and number of the box you selected from the reverse side:

Eligibility under 8 CFR 274a.12

( ) ( ) ( )

Complete the reverse of this form before signature.

Your Certification: I certify, under penalty of perjury under the laws of the United States of America, that the foregoing is true and correct. Furthermore, I authorize the release of any information which the Immigration and Naturalization Service needs to determine eligibility for the benefit I am seeking. I have read the reverse of this form and have checked the appropriate block, which is identified in item #16, above.

Signature   _Telephone Number_   _Date_

Signature of Person Preparing Form If Other Than Above: I declare that this document was prepared by me at the request of the applicant and is based on all information of which I have any knowledge.

Print Name   _Address_   _Signature_   _Date_

Initial Receipt	Resubmitted	Relocated		Completed		
		Rec'd	Sent	Approved	Denied	Returned

Form I-765 (Rev. 12/7/90) N Page 2

Eligibility

GROUP A

The current immigration laws and regulations permit certain classes of aliens to work in the United States. If you are an alien described below, you do not need to request that employment authorization be granted to you, but you do need to request a document to show that you are able to work in the United States. For aliens in classes (a) (3) through (a) (11), **NO FEE** will be required for the original card or for extension cards. A **FEE** will be required if a replacement employment authorization document is needed. A **FEE IS REQUIRED** for aliens in item (a) (12) who are over the age of 14 years and under the age of 65 years.

Place an X in the box next to the number which applies to you.

☐ (a) (3) - I have been admitted to the United States as a refugee.

☐ (a) (4) - I have been paroled into the United States as a refugee.

☐ (a) (5) - My application for asylum has been granted.

☐ (a) (6) - I am the fiancé(e) of a United States citizen and I have K-1 nonimmigrant status; OR I am the dependent of a fiancé(e) of a United States citizen and I have K-2 nonimmigrant status.

☐ (a) (7) - I have N-8 or N-9 nonimmigrant status in the United States.

☐ (a) (8) - I am a citizen of the Federated States of Micronesia or of the Marshall Islands.

☐ (a) (10) - I have been granted withholding of deportation.

☐ (a) (11) - I have been granted extended voluntary departure by the Attorney General.

☐ (a) (12) - I am an alien who has been registered for Temporary Protected Status (TPS) and I want an employment authorization document. **FEE REQUIRED.**

meaning of the International Organization Immunities Act. I have certification from this sponsor and I have also attached my INS Form I-20 ID copy. **FEE REQUIRED.**

☐ (c) (4) - I am the dependent of an officer or employee of an international organization (G-1 or G-4). I have attached certification from the Department of State recommending employment. **NO FEE.**

☐ (c) (5) - I am the dependent of an exchange visitor and I have J-2 nonimmigrant status. **FEE REQUIRED.**

☐ (c) (6) - I am a vocational foreign student (M-1). I have attached certification from the designated school official recommending employment for practical training. I have also attached my INS Form I-20ID Copy. **FEE REQUIRED.**

☐ (c) (7) - I am the dependent of an individual classified as NATO-1 through NATO-7. **FEE REQUIRED.**

☐ (c) (8) - I have filed a non-frivolous application for asylum in the United States and the application is pending. **FEE REQUIRED FOR REPLACEMENT ONLY.**

☒ (c) (9) - I have filed an application for adjustment of status to lawful permanent resident status and the application is pending. **FEE REQUIRED.**

☐ (c) (10) - I have filed an application for suspension of deportation and the application is still pending. **FEE REQUIRED.**

☐ (c) (11) - I have been paroled into the United States for emergent reasons or for reasons in the public interest. **FEE REQUIRED.**

☐ (c) (12) - I am a deportable alien and I have been granted voluntary departure either prior to or after my hearing before the immigration judge. **FEE REQUIRED.**

GROUP C

The immigration law and regulations allow certain aliens to apply for employment authorization. If you are an alien described in one of the classes below you may request employment authorization from the INS and, if granted, you will receive an employment authorization document. The instruction FEE REQUIRED printed below refers to your initial document, replacement, and extension.

Place an X in the box next to the number which applies to you.

☐ (c) (1) - I am the dependent of a foreign government official (A-1 or A-2). I have attached certification from the Department of State recommending employment. NO FEE.

☐ (c) (2) - I am the dependent of an employee of the Coordination Council of North American Affairs and I have E-1 nonimmigrant status. I have attached certification of my status from the American Institute of Taiwan. FEE REQUIRED.

☐ (c) (3) (i) - I am a foreign student (F-1). I have attached certification from the designated school official recommending employment for economic necessity. I have also attached my INS Form I-20 ID copy. FEE REQUIRED.

☐ (c) (3) (ii) - I am a foreign student (F-1). I have attached certification from the designated school official recommending employment for practical training. I have also attached my INS Form I-20 ID copy. FEE REQUIRED.

☐ (c) (3) (iii) - I am a foreign student (F-1). I have attached certification from my designated school official and I have been offered employment under the sponsorship of an international organization within the

☐ (c) (13) - I have been placed in exclusion or deportation proceedings. I have not received a final order of deportation or exclusion and I have not been detained. I understand that I must show economic necessity and I will refer to the instructions concerning "Basic Criteria to Establish Economic Necessity." FEE REQUIRED.

☐ (c) (14) - I have been granted deferred action by INS as an act of administrative convenience to the government. I understand that I must show economic necessity and I will refer to the instructions concerning "Basic Criteria to Establish Economic Necessity." FEE REQUIRED.

☐ (c) (16) - I entered the United States prior to January 1, 1972 and have been here since January 1, 1972. I have applied for registry as a lawful permanent resident alien and my application is pending. FEE REQUIRED.

☐ (c) (17) (i) - I am a (B-1) visitor for business. I am and have been (before coming to the United States) the domestic or personal servant for my employer who is temporarily in the United States. FEE REQUIRED.

☐ (c) (17) (ii) - I am a visitor for business (B-1) and am the employee of a foreign airline. I have B-1 nonimmigrant classification because I am unable to obtain visa classification as a treaty trader (E-1). FEE REQUIRED.

☐ (c) (18) - I am a deportable alien who has been placed under an order of supervision (OS). I understand that I must show economic necessity and I will refer to the instructions concerning "Basic Criteria to Establish Economic Necessity." FEE REQUIRED.

☐ (c) (19) - I am an alien who is prima facie eligible for Temporary Protected Status (TPS) and (1) INS has not given me a reasonable chance to register during the first 30 days of the registration period [FEE REQUIRED], or (2) INS has not made a final decision as to my eligibility for TPS. FEE REQUIRED.

FPI-PET

GPO : 1991 0 - 289-028 (40046)

PLEASE DO NOT STAPLE THIS FORM

**ASSURE THAT IMPRESSIONS ON
ALL COPIES ARE CLEAR**

APPROVED OMB 3116-0006 EXP. 10/31/92
*Estimated Burden Hours: 15 mins. (See page 4).

D 328144

United States Information Agency
EXCHANGE VISITOR FACILITATIVE STAFF GC/V
CERTIFICATE OF ELIGIBILITY FOR EXCHANGE VISITOR (J-1) STATUS

1 _____   ( ) Male
   (FAMILY NAME OF EXCHANGE VISITOR)   (FIRST NAME)   (MIDDLE NAME)   ( ) Female

born ____ ____ ____ in _____   _____
     (Mo.) (Day) (Yr.)   (City)   (Country)

a citizen of _____
             (Country)

_____, a legal permanent resident of _____
     (Code)

_____, whose position in that country is _____
     (Country)   (Code)

_____
(Pos. Code)

U.S. address _____

2 will be sponsored by _____

_____ to participate in Exchange Visitor Program No. _____, which is still valid and is officially described as follows:

3 This form covers the period from ____ ____ ____ to ____ ____ ____ Students are permitted to travel abroad & maintain status (e.g. obtain a new visa)
                                   (Mo.) (Day) (Yr.)   (Mo.) (Day) (Yr.)
under duration of the program as indicated by the dates on this from.
If this form is for family travel or replaces a lost form, the expiration date on the exchange visitor's form in

THE PURPOSE OF THIS FORM IS TO:

1 ( ) Begin a new program ( ) Accompanied by
        ____ immediate family members

2 ( ) Extend an on-going program.

3 ( ) Transfer to a different program

4 ( ) Replace a lost form.

5 ( ) Permit visitor's immediate family
        (____ members) to enter U.S. separately.

SAMPLE FORM

4. The category of this visitor is 1 ( ) Student, 2 ( ) Trainee, 3 ( ) Teacher, 4 ( ) Professor, Research Scholar or Specialist, 5 ( ) International Visitor, 6 ( ) Medical Trainee, 7 ( ) Alien employee of the USIA. The Specific field of study, research training or professional activity is _____ verbally described as follows:

(Subj/Field Code)

5. During the period covered by this form, it is estimated that the following financial support (in U.S. $) will be provided to this exchange visitor by:

a ( ) The Program Sponsor in item 2 above $ _____

This Program Sponsor has ☐ has not ☐ (check one) received funding for international exchange from one or more U.S. Government Agency(ies) to support this exchange visitor. If any U.S. Government Agency(ies) provided funding, indicate the Agency(ies) by code _____.

Financial support from organizations other than the sponsor will be provided by one or more of the following:

b1. ( ) U.S. Government Agency(ies): _____ (Agency Code). b2. _____ $ _____ (Agency Code).

c1. ( ) International Organization(s): _____ (Int. Org. Code). c2. _____ $ _____ (Int. Org. Code).

d. ( ) The Exchange Visitor's Government $ _____   (If necessary, use above spaces
e. ( ) The binational Commission of the visitor's Country $ _____   for funding by multiple U.S.
f. ( ) All other organizations providing support $ _____   Agencies or Intl. Organizations)
g. ( ) Personal funds $ _____

6. I.N.S. USE

7. _____
   (Name of Official Preparing Form)

   _____
   (Address)

   _____
   (Signature of Responsible Officer or Alternate R.O.)

8. **STATEMENT OF RESPONSIBLE OFFICER FOR RELEASING SPONSOR (FOR TRANSFER OF PROGRAM)**

   Date _____. Transfer of this exchange visitor from program No. _____ sponsored by _____ to the program specified in item (2) is necessary or highly desirable and is in conformity with the objectives of the Mutual Educational and Cultural Exchange Act of 1961.

   _____   _____   _____
   (Signature of Officer)   *(Title)*   *(Date)*

PRELIMINARY ENDORSEMENT OF CONSULAR OR IMMIGRATION OFFICER REGARDING SECTION 212 (e) OF THE I.N.S.

I _____ (Name)
_____ (Title)

have determined that this alien in the above program

1 ( ) is not subject to the two year residence requirement
2 ( ) is subject based on — A ( ) government financing and/or
                             B ( ) the Exchange visitor skills list and/or
                             C ( ) PL 94 484 as amended

The United States Information Agency reserves the right to make the final determination

_____   _____
(Signature of Officer)   *(Date)*

IAP-66 (12-90)   Copy 1 - For Immigration and Naturalization Service   PAGE 1

INSTRUCTIONS FOR AND CERTIFICATION BY the alien beneficiary named on page 1 of this Form:

Read and complete this page prior to presentation to a United States consular or immigration official.

1.   I understand that the following conditions are applicable to exchange visitors:

(a)   *Extension of Stay and Program Transfers.* A completed form IAP-66 is required in order to apply for an extension or transfer and may be obtained from or with the assistance of the sponsor. It must be sumitted to the appropriate office of the Immigration and Naturalization Service within fifteen to sixty days before the expiration of the authorized period of stay.

(b)   *Limitation on Stay:* STUDENTS -as long as they pursue a substantial scholastic program leading to recognized degrees or certificate. Students for whom the sponsor recommends practical training may be permitted to remain for such purpose for an additional period of up to 18 months after receiving their degree or certificate. BUSINESS AND INDUSTRIAL TRAINEES - 18 months. TEACHERS, PROFESSORS, RESEARCH SCHOLARS, and SPECIALISTS - 3 years. INTERNATIONAL VISITORS - 1 year. MEDICAL TRAINEES: Graduate Nurses - 2 years. Medical Technologists, Medical Record Librarians, Medical Record Technicians, Radiologic Technicians, and other participants in similar categories - the length of the approved training program plus a maximum of 18 months for practical experience, not exceeding a total of 3 years. Medical Interns and Residents - the time typically required to complete the medical specialty involved but limited to 7 years with the possibility of extension if such extension is approved by the Director of the United States Information Agency.

(c)   *Documentation Required for Admission or Readmission as an Exchange Visitor:* To be eligible for admission or readmission to the United States, an exchange visitor must present the following at the port of entry: (1) A valid nonimmigrant visa bearing classification J-1, unless exempt from nonimmigrant visa requirements; (2) A passport valid for six months beyond the anticipated period of admission, unless exempt from passport requirements; (3) A properly executed Form IAP-66. Copies one and two of Form IAP-66 must be surrendered to a United States immigration officer upon arrival in the United States. Copy three may be retained for re-entries within a period of previously authorized stay.

(d)   *Change of Status:* Exchange visitors are expected to leave the United States upon completing their objective. An exchange visitor who is subject to the two-year home-country physical presence requirement is not eligible to change his/her status while in the United States to any other nonimmigrant category except, if applicable, that of official or employee of a foreign government (A) or of an international organization (G) or member of the family or attendant of either of these types of officials or employees.

(e)   *Two-Year Home Country Physical Presence Requirement:* Any exchange visitor whose program is financed in whole or in part, directly or indirectly by either his/her own government or by the United States Government is required to reside in his/her own country for two years following completion of his/her program in the United States before he/she can become eligible for permanent residence (immigration) or for status as a temporary worker ("H") or as an intracompany transferee ("L"). Likewise, if an exchange visitor is acquiring a skill which is in short supply in his/her own country (these skills appear on the

Exchange Visitor Skills List) he/she will be subject to this same two-year home-country residence requirement as well as alien physicians entering the U.S. to receive graduate medical education or training (Section 212(e) of the Immigration and Nationality Act and PL 94 484 as amended).

2. I seek to enter into, or remain temporarily in, the United States as an exchange visitor under Section 101(a)(15)(J) of the Immigration and Nationality Act, as amended, for a total maximum stay of _____ *(months or years)* for the purpose of *(state type of degree, certificate, or other objective toward which your program participation will be directed. Doctors of medicine should indicate their medical specialty):* _____

and I understand that I shall be permitted to perform only those activities described in Item 2 and 4 on page 1 of this Form.

I intend to return to (country) _____ where I am (check one) ☐ legal permanent resident ☐ citizen.

3. My passport numbered _____ issued by _____ (Country) expires on _____
_____ (Mo./Day/Yr.)

4. I ☐ have ☐ have not *(check one)* been in the United States previously as an exchange visitor. (If you have been in the United States previously as an exchange visitor, show total length of time: _____ , and dates: _____):

5. (To be completed only if application is being made for extension of stay or Program transfer. Use a continuation sheet if necessary.) I first entered the United States as an exchange visitor, or acquired exchange visitor status, on _____ *(Mo./Day/Yr.)* and have engaged in the following activities under the sponsorship of respective institutions listed for each activity *(include program numbers)*.

6. I understand that a consular or Immigration Officer will make a preliminary determination on whether I am subject to the two year home country physical present requirement described in item 1(e) above. The United States Information Agency reserves the right to make a final determination. When determined subject, I will accept that determination and comply with the requirement.

7. I certify that I have read and I understand the foregoing.

_____ _____ _____
(Signature of Applicant) *(Place)* *(Date: Mo. Day, Yr.)*

IAP-66 (12-90)

INSTRUCTIONS FOR AND CERTIFICATION BY the alien beneficiary named on page 1 of this Form:

Read and complete this page prior to presentation to a United States consular or immigration official.

1. I understand that the following conditions are applicable to exchange visitors:

(a) *Extension of Stay and Program Transfers.* A completed form IAP-66 is required in order to effect an extension or transfer and may be obtained from or with the assistance of the sponsor. It must be submitted to the appropriate office of the Immigration and Naturalization Service within fifteen to sixty days before the expiration of the authorized period of stay.

(b) *Limitation on Stay:* STUDENTS -as long as they pursue a substantial scholastic program leading to recognized degrees or certificate. Students for whom the sponsor recommends practical training may be permitted to remain for such purpose for an additional period of up to 18 months after receiving their degree or certificate. BUSINESS AND INDUSTRIAL TRAINEES - 18 months. TEACHERS, PROFESSORS, RESEARCH SCHOLARS, and SPECIALISTS - 3 years. INTERNATIONAL VISITORS - 1 year. MEDICAL TRAINEES: Graduate Nurses - 2 years. Medical Technologists, Medical Record Librarians, Medical Record Technicians, Radiologic Technicians, and other participants in similar categories - the length of the approved training program plus a maximum of 18 months for practical experience, not exceeding a total of 3 years. Medical Interns and Residents - the time typically required to complete the medical specialty involved but limited to 7 years with the possibility of extension if such extension is approved by the Director of the United States Information Agency.

(c) *Documentation Required for Admission or Readmission as an Exchange Visitor:* To be eligible for admission or readmission to the United States, an exchange visitor must present the following at the port of entry: (1) A valid nonimmigrant visa bearing classification J-1, unless exempt from nonimmigrant visa requirements; (2) A passport valid for six months beyond the anticipated period of admission, unless exempt from passport requirements; (3) A properly executed Form IAP-66. Copies one and two of Form IAP-66 must be surrendered to a United States immigration officer upon arrival in the United States. Copy three may be retained for re-entries within a period of previously authorized stay.

(d) *Change of Status:* Exchange visitors are expected to leave the United States upon completing their objective. An exchange visitor who is subject to the two-year home-country physical presence requirement is not eligible to change his/her status while in the United States to any other nonimmigrant category except, if applicable, that of official or employee of a foreign government (A) or of an international organization (G) or member of the family or attendant of either of these types of officials or employees.

(e) *Two-Year Home Country Physical Presence Requirement:* Any exchange visitor whose program is financed in whole or in part, directly or indirectly by either his/her own government or by the United States Government is required to reside in his/her own country for two years following completion of his/her program in the United States before he/she can become eligible for permanent residence (immigration) or for status as a temporary worker ("H") or as an intracompany transferee ("L"). Likewise, if an exchange visitor is acquiring a skill which is in short supply in his/her own country (these skills appear on the *Exchange Visitor Skills List*) he/she will be subject to this same two-year home-country residence requirement as well as alien physicians entering the U.S. to receive graduate medical education or training (Section 212(e) of the Immigration and Nationality Act and PL 94-484, as amended).

(Signature of Applicant) _(Place)_ _(Date: Mo., Day, Yr.)_

IAP-66 (12-85)

NOTICE TO ALL EXCHANGE VISITORS

To facilitate your readmission to the United States after a visit to another country other than a contiguous territory or adjacent islands you should have the Responsible Officer of your sponsoring organization indicate that you continue to be in good standing on this copy of the IAP-66 form.

VALIDATION BY RESPONSIBLE OFFICER

(1) Exchange visitor is in good standing from ⸻ to ⸻

Signature of Responsible Officer

(2) Exchange visitor is in good standing from ⸻ to ⸻

Signature of Responsible Officer

(3) Exchange visitor is in good standing from ⸻ to ⸻

Signature of Responsible Officer

(4) Exchange visitor is in good standing from ⸻ to ⸻

Signature of Responsible Officer

(5) Exchange visitor is in good standing from ⸻ to ⸻

Signature of Responsible Officer

THIS FORM IS SUPPLIED GRATIS

NONIMMIGRANT VISA INFORMATION

I. IMPORTANT INFORMATION

Effective July 1, 1988, British citizens do not require visas for the United States if they meet certain requirements.

WHO MAY TRAVEL WITHOUT A VISA

Travelers who meet <u>ALL</u> of the following requirements NO LONGER NEED A VISA FOR TRAVEL TO THE UNITED STATES:

- the traveler is a BRITISH CITIZEN, with full right of abode in the United Kingdom and traveling on an unexpired BRITISH passport; or a citizen of Japan, France, Switzerland, Germany, Italy, Sweden, Netherlands, Spain, Austria, New Zealand, Finland, Belgium, Denmark, Norway, Iceland, Luxembourg, San Marino, Andorra, Monaco and Leichtenstein;

- the trip is for holiday or business;

- the trip is for 90 days or less;

- if entering by air or sea, the traveler must have a return or onward ticket for a destination outside of North America and adjacent islands and must enter aboard an air or sea carrier participating in the Visa Waiver Program. If entering by land, no onward or return ticket is required.

WHO STILL NEEDS A VISA

If ANY of the following circumstances apply, the traveler <u>MUST apply for a visa</u>:

- the trip is for any purpose other than holiday or business (eg. government officials traveling on official business, students undertaking a course of study in the U.S., temporary workers, journalists on assignment, exchange visitors, treaty traders and investors, intra-company transferees, fiance(e)s of U.S. citizens, crew members, and transit passengers require visas);

- the trip is for more than 90 days

- the traveler has a British passport but is not a British citizen with full right of abode, i.e. the traveler is a British Dependent Territories citizen, British Overseas citizen, British National (Overseas) citizen or British subject only;

- If the traveler has been refused a visa or previously been denied admission to the U.S. or required to leave by the U.S. Immigration and Naturalization Service, he or she should contact the Embassy prior to attempting to travel without a visa.

VISA VALIDITY

A United States visa is only valid for the purpose for which it was issued. For example, a student visa cannot be used for entry as a temporary worker.

The validity period shown on a non-immigrant visa refers only to the period during which it may be used to make application to enter the United States. It does not indicate the length of time the traveler may remain in the U.S.

ADMISSION

A VISA IS NOT A GUARANTEE OF ENTRY INTO THE UNITED STATES. When a traveler reaches the United States, an Immigration and Naturalization Service Officer determines whether or not a person qualifies under law to enter the U.S. This applies whether the traveler has a visa or not. Therefore, travelers should carry with them evidence of the purpose of the trip, evidence of funds to support themselves during the stay in the U.S., and evidence of plans to leave the U.S. after a reasonable stay.

WORKING IN THE UNITED STATES

ONLY holders of special work visas may work in the United States. Holders of other types of visas may not accept employment, even informal work work in a household as a "nanny", "au-pair", or "Mothers Helper".

FEES FOR VISAS

There is no charge for most visas for British citizens. If your type of visa requires a fee, you will be notified of the amount and how to pay it.

IMPORTANT - TURN OVER PAGE FOR DETAILS

If you qualify for travel without a visa, you need not submit this application. If your trip requires a visa, simply follow these steps :

1) Complete both sides of the attached application form, printing clearly. Sign the application. If several family members travel on a single passport, complete an application for each person, even babies.

2) Photograph. If you are over 16, staple a small photograph to the back of the application.

3) Submit evidence substantiating the purpose of your trip and your intention to depart from the United States after a temporary visit. Examples of such evidence are: in cases of business trips, a letter from your employer; in cases of pleasure trips, documents outlining your plans while in the United States and explaining the reasons why you would return abroad after a short stay, such as family ties, employment, or similar binding obligations in your home country; for students a completed form I-20 A/B; for exchange visitors a form IAP-66; and for temporary workers and intra-company transferees, evidence of an approved petition.

4) If you are a British Citizen or U.K. resident, you may post your completed application form, your passport (British Visitor's Passports are not acceptable), any supporting documents and a STAMPED, ADDRESSED ENVELOPE.

5) Allow three weeks for processing your application. Your passport will be returned to you in the stamped, addressed envelope you provide. If you fail to provide a stamped addressed envelope, your visa application is subject to considerable delay.

Residents of England, Scotland and Wales should apply to:

        Visa Branch, United States Embassy

        5 Upper Grosvenor Street, London   W1A 2JB

Residents of Northern Ireland should apply to:

        United States Consulate General

        Queen's House, Queen Street, Belfast BT1 6EQ

As of July 8, 1988 the U.S. Consulate General, Edinburgh, no longer processes any visa applications.

6) Applicants who are not eligible to travel without a visa may request an appointment for an interview through the mail, by telephone (081 205 7090) or in person.

7) All applicants who are not residents of the U.K. must request an interview.

IMPORTANT: Under United States law, some people are ineligible to enter the U.S., unless they first obtain a waiver of ineligibility and a visa. If any condition noted in item 34 applies to you, you should submit a visa application BEFORE you make final travel plans. The U.S. Government cannot accept responsibility for any charges you incur if we are unable to issue a visa or if you are not admitted to the U.S.

For additional information, call 0898 200 290.

HOLIDAY NOTICE

Consular offices are closed on British and American holidays. If a holiday falls on a Saturday, the consular office will close on the preceding Friday. If a holiday is on a Sunday, consular offices will close on the following Monday. We suggest you do not apply the day after an American holiday as it is always busier than usual. The following are American holidays:

January 1	- New Years Day	First Monday of September	- Labor Day
Third Monday of January	- Martin Luther King's Birthday	Second Monday of October	- Columbus Day
Third Monday of February	- Washington's Brithday	November 11	- Veterans Day
Last Monday of May	- Memorial Day	Fourth Thursday of November	- Thanksgiving Day
July 4	- Independence Day	December 25	- Christmas Day

MEDICAL CARE IN THE UNITED STATES

Medical Care in the United States is expensive and must be paid for if required, even in cases of emergency. Serious injury or major illness requiring specialized treatment and/or prolonged hospitalization will incur costs which may be far in excess of the normal health insurance cover offered by airlines or tour companies. Since provision for meeting such costs is the responsibility of the individual, you may wish to consider obtaining health insurance sufficient to cover such eventualities occurring during your visit. Your travel agent or insurance broker will be able to advise you.

THIS FORM IS SUPPLIED GRATIS

21-0192

PLEASE TYPE OR PRINT YOUR ANSWERS IN THE SPACE PROVIDED BELOW EACH ITEM

1. SURNAMES OR FAMILY NAMES (Exactly as in Passport)

DO NOT WRITE IN THIS SPACE

2. FIRST NAME AND MIDDLE NAME (Exactly as in Passport)

3. OTHER NAMES (Maiden, Religious, Professional, Aliases)

4. DATE OF BIRTH (Day, Month, Year)

8. PASSPORT NUMBER

5. PLACE OF BIRTH
City, Province   Country

DATE PASSPORT ISSUED
(Day, Month, Year)

6. NATIONALITY   7. SEX

☐ Male
☐ Female

DATE PASSPORT EXPIRES
(Day, Month, Year)

9. HOME ADDRESS (include apartment no., street, city, province and postal zone)

10. NAME AND STREET ADDRESS OF PRESENT EMPLOYER OR SCHOOL
(Postal Box number unacceptable)

11. HOME TELEPHONE NO.   12. BUSINESS TELEPHONE NO.

13. COLOR OF HAIR   14. COLOR OF EYES   15. COMPLEXION

16. HEIGHT   17. MARKS OF IDENTIFICATION

24. PRESENT OCCUPATION (If retired state past occupation)

18. MARITAL STATUS
☐ Married ☐ Single ☐ Widowed ☐ Divorced ☐ Separated
If married, give name and nationality of spouse

19. NAMES AND RELATIONSHIPS OF PERSONS TRAVELING WITH YOU
(NOTE: A separate application must be made for each visa traveler, regardless of age.)

20. HAVE YOU EVER APPLIED FOR A U.S. VISA BEFORE, WHETHER IMMIGRANT OR NON-IMMIGRANT?
☐ No
☐ Yes
When ? _____ Where ? _____ Type of Visa ? _____
☐ Visa was issued ☐ Visa was refused

21. HAS YOUR U.S. VISA EVER BEEN CANCELED?
☐ No
☐ Yes
When ? _____ Where ? _____ By Whom ? _____

22. Bearers of visitors visas may generally not work or study in the U.S.
DO YOU INTEND TO WORK IN THE U.S.? ☐ No ☐ Yes
If YES, explain

23. DO YOU INTEND TO STUDY IN THE U.S. ? ☐ No ☐ Yes
If YES, write name and address of school as it appears on form I-20.

25. WHO WILL FURNISH FINANCIAL SUPPORT, INCLUDING TICKETS ?

26. AT WHAT ADDRESS WILL YOU STAY IN THE USA?

27. WHAT IS THE PURPOSE OF YOUR TRIP ?

28. WHEN DO YOU INTEND TO ARRIVE IN THE USA?

29. HOW LONG DO YOU PLAN TO STAY IN THE USA?

30. HAVE YOU EVER BEEN IN THE USA ?
☐ No
☐ Yes When? _____
For How long ? _____

NONIMMIGRANT VISA APPLICATION

COMPLETE ALL QUESTIONS ON REVERSE OF FORM

OPTIONAL FORM 156 (Rev 4-91) PAGE 1   50156-106
Department of State

NSN 7540-00-139-0053

31. (a) HAVE YOU OR ANYONE ACTING FOR YOU EVER INDICATED TO A U.S. CONSULAR OR IMMIGRATION EMPLOYEE A DESIRE TO IMMIGRATE TO THE U.S.? (b) HAS ANYONE EVER FILED AN IMMIGRANT VISA PETITION ON YOUR BEHALF? (C) HAS LABOR CERTIFICATION FOR EMPLOYMENT IN THE U.S. EVER BEEN REQUESTED BY YOU OR ON YOUR BEHALF?

(a) ☐No ☐Yes   (b) ☐No ☐Yes   (c) ☐No ☐Yes

32. ARE ANY OF THE FOLLOWING IN THE U.S.? (If YES, circle appropriate relationship and indicate that person's status in the U.S., ie. studying, working, U.S. permenant resident, U.S. citizen, etc.)

HUSBAND/WIFE _____ FIANCE/FIANCEE _____ BROTHER/SISTER _____

FATHER/MOTHER _____ SON/DAUGHTER _____

33. PLEASE LIST THE COUNTRIES WHERE YOU HAVE LIVED FOR MORE THAN 6 MONTHS DURING THE PAST 5 YEARS. BEGIN WITH YOUR PRESENT RESIDENCE.

<u>Countries</u>   <u>Cities</u>   <u>Approximate Dates</u>

_____

34. IMPORTANT: ALL APPLICANTS MUST READ AND CHECK THE APPROPRIATE BOX FOR EACH ITEM:

A visa may not be issued to persons who are within specific categories defined by law as inadmissable to the United States (except when a waiver is obtained in advance). Are any of the following applicable to you?

– Have you ever been afflicted with a communicable disease of public health significance, a
dangerous physical or mental disorder, or been a drug abuser or addict? .... ☐Yes ☐No

– Have you ever been arrested or convicted for any offense or crime, even through subject of a
pardon, amnesty, or other such legal action? .... ☐Yes ☐No

– Have you ever been a controlled substance (drug) trafficker, or a prostitute or procurer? .... ☐Yes ☐No

– Have you ever sought to obtain, or assist others to obtain a visa, entry into the U.S., or any U.S.
immigration benefit by fraud or willful misrepresentation? .... ☐Yes ☐No

– Were you deported from the U.S.A. within the last 5 years? .... ☐Yes ☐No

— Do you seek to enter the United States to engage in export control violations, subversive or terrorist activities or any unlawful purpose? .... ☐Yes ☐No

— Have you ever ordered, incited, assisted, or otherwise participated in the persecution of any person because of race, religion, national origin, or political opinion under the control, direct or indirect, of the Nazi Government of Germany, or of the government of any area occupied by, or allied with, the Nazi Government of Germany, or have you ever participated in genocide?.......... ☐Yes ☐No

A YES answer does not automatically signify ineligibility for a visa, but if you answered YES to any of the above, or if you have any question in this regard, personal appearance at this office is recommended. If appearance is not possible at this time, attach a statement of facts in your case to this application.

35. I certify that I have read and understood all the questions set forth in this application and the answers I have furnished on this form are true and correct to the best of my knowledge and belief. I understand that any false or misleading statement may result in the permanent refusal of a visa or denial of entry into the United States. I understand that possession of a visa does not entitle the bearer to enter the United States of America upon arrival at port of entry if he or she is found inadmissable.

DATE OF APPLICATION _____

APPLICANT'S SIGNATURE _____

If this application has been prepared by a travel agency or another person on your behalf, the agent should indicate name and address of agency or person with appropriate signature of individual preparing form.

SIGNATURE OF PERSON PREPARING FORM _____
(If other than the applicant)

DO NOT WRITE IN THIS SPACE

37mm x 37mm

——PHOTO——

Glue or Staple
photo here

Optional Form 156 (Rev. 4-91) PAGE 2
Department of State

INDEX